Teaching History Series 49

The Visual Dimension in the Study and Teaching of History

by: Robert Unwin, BA, PhD, PhD

published by

THE HISTORICAL ASSOCIATION

59a Kennington Park Road, London, SE11 4JH

ACKNOWLEDGEMENTS

I wish to express my appreciation of the help and advice I received from Miss Margaret Bryant and Mr. J. Hunt, who gave me the benefit of their opinion of the text when it was in draft form. Thanks also to Miss Christine Povall, who has seen the manuscript through to publication, and to Barbara Carthew who has typed it. Above all, my appreciation to Pat, without whom this study would have been impossible.

R.W. Unwin,
Leeds University,
September 1981

Originated by The Historical Association, 59a Kennington Park Road, London SE11 4JH and printed in Great Britain by The Chameleon Press Limited, 5-25 Burr Road, London SW18 4SG HA 2.0981

ISBN 0 85278 241 1

CONTENTS

ILLUSTRATIONS

Front cover illustration: This scene from Froissart's *Chronicles*, which is reproduced by kind permission of The Mansell Collection, shows two episodes on 15 June 1381 in a single illustration. On the left, at Smithfield, Richard II looks on as Walworth the mayor strikes Wat Tyler. On the right, Richard offers himself to the rebels as their chief and captain. From Les *Chroniques* de Jehan Froissart (c.1338-1410).

KEY 1 Richard II; 2 Wat Tyler; 3 Walworth; 4 Rebels.

Back cover illustration: Eight hundred and fifty years later, the Bayeux Tapestry is revived in a pull-out cartoon - a piece of English propaganda showing Wilhelm the non-Conqueror; reproduced by kind permission of The British Library.

page 24	*Aerial Photographs of Wetherby* by kind permission of Aerofilms Limited
page 30	*Gin Lane and Beer Street* reproduced from photographs by kind permission of John R. Freeman & Company
page 32	*The Fellow 'Prentices* reproduced from a photograph by kind permission of John R. Freeman & Company
page 40	*Football 'cropping'* reproduced by kind permission of Yorkshire Post Newspapers
pages 42 & 43	Scenes from *The Bayeux Tapestry* reproduced by kind permission of the Victoria & Albert Museum
page 60	*Sheffield 1900 and 1970* reproduced by kind permission of Sheffield City Library
page 62	*Two views of Cotton Mills* reproduced by kind permission of Radio Times Hulton Picture Library

INTRODUCTION: PURPOSE OF THE PAMPHLET

A few years ago, the view was held by many history teachers that there was a shortage of well-illustrated material for class use. This has now changed and today a greater range of visual sources is available.(1) Literature has tended to atrophy our visual awareness, often in a restrictive puritan way, but now the balance is being restored, and a growing number of professional historians place some reliance on the use of visual evidence. Introducing *The Age of Experience*, H. Trevor-Roper explained that

> *Faced by the vast expansion of our field, we have called in the new world of photographic reproduction, which informs through the eyes to redress the imbalance of the old purely literary method ... and by its illustrations not merely to enliven but to deepen the study and understanding of that history.(2)*

The development of photography as a significant alternative method of historical recording and the widespread impact of cinema and television, which have produced a cultural situation less dependent on the written or printed word, have significant implications for both pedagogy and research, increasing value being placed on the visual dimension for all periods.(3)

A widely held - or at least often expressed - view is that the visual image has now largely replaced the written word as our principal means of communication, although much of the talk about the impact of the mass media lacks historical perspective. For example, even during the struggle for working-class literacy, when every word mattered, pictures - broadsheets, pamphlets, cartoons, trade union emblems - played a role too.(4) Greater attention to the visual sources of history is partly justified by the value which they had for contemporaries.

Changes in reprographic technology and pedagogical approaches help to explain the proliferation of visual material in the classroom, but here too there are dangers in overplaying the 'enlightenment' of the present generation. The illustration of texts, pictorial biographies, and published collections of photographs, to cite three broad categories of visual material, are not recent trends. In the inter-war years the Quennells, in the *Everyday Life* series, made extensive use of visual reconstructions and may almost be said to have developed a new way of writing history for children. Although widely praised, the extensive use of line drawings and reconstructions was not universally accepted, and purists insisted that even the most careful redrawing of contemporary pictures led to some degree of falsification. Critics of artists' imaginings and restorations argued that children were sensitive to subtle nuances of visual expression and that the modernity of the hand would betray itself and destroy the vivid reality of the original illustrations. Doubting the value of modern visual transcripts, two London schoolteachers based the four-volume *Life and Work of the People of England* (1929) on contemporary prints, engravings and drawings reproduced photographically, and attempted to illustrate the history of a period 'through the eyes of the people who lived in it'.(5) Emphasising that original pictures were a mine of inexhaustible detail, the authors argued that contemporary illustrations represented the life of a period in a manner unsurpassed for vivid interpretation and graphic power and with greater artistic vigour than modern line drawings and reconstructions.

Pictorial biographies also have a longer pedigree than might perhaps be supposed, but when *The Pictorial Life of Wolfe* was published in 1927 it was claimed that 'the novelty of the book centres in its wealth of illustrations.(6) Where documentary evidence is scanty, it has been recognised for some years that much can be gained by a pictorial approach, exemplified in *In Search of Christopher Marlowe* (1965) and *Sir Francis Drake: A Pictorial Biography* (1970).(7)

The first documentary photographs (unfortunately lost) were probably the Daguerreotypes taken to illustrate Mayhew's *London Labour and the London Poor* (1851), while the journalistic photo-interview was initiated by Tournachan and Nadar as long ago as 1886.(8) Many albums of nineteenth century photographs have been published, sometimes of great aesthetic worth and documentary value. What is perhaps new today is the conviction that such collections possess a unique educative value, and that by looking at visual sources one can obtain an understanding of a period or place which goes beyond anything the written word can offer. When pictures are 'frozen', for example in the work of Charles Nègre in Paris, D.O. Hill in Edinburgh, William Notman in Montreal, or in collections such as *Early Photography in Canada*, the marvellous sense of arrested time is likely to be lost if they are blandly praised simply as 'delightful in themselves'.(9) There is a danger that the period evocation of photographs will cloud objective criticism both with a romantic nostalgia and with the appeal of 'genuine historical revelation'. Thus it can be argued that the extent to which the full value of a collection of old photographs is realised depends less upon the actual photographs than upon the quality of the editorial guidance that is offered.

Just as one needs to be taught to read if the written word is not to remain an unsolved mystery, it is equally important that attention is given to the visual 'still' - whether this is photograph or portrait; cartoon or comic; tapestry or text-book illustration; advertisement or artist's reconstruction. It may be possible too for the historian to consider the advantages of employing a 'rationale for looking', for, as Professor McCord has argued

> *If we study a photograph of a late nineteenth-century family or an early twentieth-century school group - if indeed we study old photographs of any kind of individual or group and try to draw historical conclusions from them - then we are using precisely the same approach to historical understanding as that employed by the archaeologist who tries to understand the Roman or Dacian armies from reliefs on Trajan's column, or tries to piece together something of early medieval Chinese society from paintings on the walls of eighth-century tombs.(10)*

For the history teacher it is becoming a matter of some urgency that more attention should be given to the problems and the possibilities of visual sources. At a time when visual information is proliferating so rapidly, it is hardly surprising that terms such as 'visual literacy' and 'graphicacy' are being used increasingly in all fields of education. If it is accepted that one of the abilities which can be fostered by a study of history is to doubt what has previously been accepted as truth, then this has implications for the whole range of evidence, so that:

> *If we are concerned to train pupils not to believe what they read, in this age it is equally important to train them not to believe their eyes or ears.(11)*

It has also been suggested that media use in history teaching will achieve greater potential when a sound theoretical justification is made in terms of the logic of the subject, or of a different pedagogy.(12)

It is the purpose of this pamphlet to consider some of the ways in which visual materials may be used by researchers and teachers. The use of media and sources covered elsewhere in the series has been explicitly excluded, while constraints of space have precluded certain kinds of graphics, flow charts and most maps.(13) Despite the increasing use of film materials, artefacts and primary visual sources, many history teachers encounter illustrations mainly in published book form, and the paper concentrates largely on the two-dimensional material most readily available for school use. Having discussed the advantages and pitfalls of establishing a rationale for looking at a wide range of visual material, the pamphlet will consider the principal categories of illustrated material before looking at the implications for history in school.

A RATIONALE FOR LOOKING INTO VISUAL EVIDENCE

The historian will search in vain for a generally accepted theoretical framework on which to base interpretations of art. Notoriously, Plato would have barred artists from his ideal state; Hume placed art on one side as irrational fantasy, the product of uncontrolled emotion; while Kant put art on an aesthetic pedestal and suggested that neither art nor the pleasure art gives need to be explained in terms of function. Art is purposeless and aesthetic pleasure is 'disinterested', so that answers to questions like 'what is art for?' or 'what does art do?' can only be found in the nature of aesthetic experience itself. Even the philosopher's general theory of the aesthetic experience insists that it is a response to a particular work of art.

It may be argued that historians are not primarily concerned with the aesthetic qualities of the evidence they use, but it is doubtful if full use can be made of visual sources without the development of some of the aesthetic sensibilities of the art critic. The historian is interested in how the artist perceives the world and in how the world wants to be perceived - its self-image. An artistic work provides the creator's image of reality, and its form may be as revealing as its content. The fundamental questions are whether such representations are 'reliable'; and how or why an artist (or school of painters) chose to represent them. An essential element of the history of art is attribution and dating, which are also essential to the historian, for the utility of a work of art as evidence is frail unless it is known when it was produced and by whom. Identification of form, classification, dating and attribution may provide the first stages in the development of a 'rationale for looking'.

Looking into visual evidence, the historian must try to discover whether the artist is making a representational or non-representational - allegorical - statement. The core of the problem of visual evidence for the historian is the relationship between those who create and those who perceive, that is, relating the visual material to the physical and mental world to which it originally belonged.(14) The historian will need to ask what situation the visual evidence was designed to illustrate or promote, what forces brought it into existence, and the circumstances in which works were produced and their effect. At the same time, an attempt must be made to understand something of the social and artistic conventions, intellectual equipment and technical skills which went into the making of the visual evidence under scrutiny.(15) If possible, an insight into the quality of the artist's imagination and of his or her feelings about his or her own place in history and the community may be helpful; in this the historian may be assisted by the aesthetic critic. In an attempt to resolve the clash between historians like Taine who argued that art was directly influenced by the political and economic upheavals of its period; and those who asserted - like Wölfflin - that works of art 'develop according to their own internal laws', Sir Kenneth Clark emphasised the validity of combining both methods of interpretation.(16) By considering the 'internal life of forms' as well as the relation of such forms to life, Clark hoped there might be revealed

> *certain workings of the historical process more subtly ... and perhaps more truthfully, than is possible in any other way.(17)*

In seeking to determine the meaning of visual evidence, the approaches of art historian and general historian are not dissimilar. Addressing the Warburg

RATIONALE FOR LOOKING INTO VISUAL EVIDENCE

Process	*Lines of Inquiry*
Identification/Authenticity	What is the form of the image? Is it true? Is it a copy? Could it be a fake?
Classification	Was it commissioned or patronized?
Dating	When was the image produced? Is it contemporary with the people/events depicted?
Attribution	Who produced the image? Why and how was the image produced? What was the viewpoint of the creator?
Examination of image statement	Is it a representational or non-representational image?
Denotation	What can be identified in the image? What patterns can be seen - objects, people, places, actions/gestures? If the image tells a story what is it about? Does the visual evidence fit the known facts from other sources? Does the creator exaggerate? Does the picture/image seem to give a true view of people/events?
Connotation	What symbolic meaning may be implied by elements within the image? Why was the image presented in the way it was? What patterns can be seen?
Recognition of pattern-break	What enigmas or problems are presented? Are there any elements that do not seem to 'fit'?
Contemporary perceiver expectation	What evidence can be found that the image did/did not meet contemporary expectations? Was the image the subject of any controversy?
Questioning	Why were contemporaries 'shocked'? What questions might they have asked?
Hypothesis construction	How did contemporaries attempt to explain images? How can they be explained today?
Explanation (which may be revised in the light of new evidence)	On what grounds can explanations of hypotheses be regarded as being satisfactory?

Institute in 1961, Professor Ettlinger stressed that

> *The art historian will have to check what he thinks is the intrinsic meaning of the work, or group of works, to which he devotes his attention, against what he thinks is the intrinsic meaning of as many other documents of civilization historically related to that work*

or group of works as he can muster: of documents bearing witness to the political, poetical, religious, philosophical and social tendencies of the personality, period or country under investigation.

It may be tempting to look merely for correlations between social conditions and art, but there are dangers in overstressing the sociological at the expense of the psychological dimension. Thus Richard Wollheim maintains that

even if such correlations were produced, explanation in terms of them would not be satisfying. For in relating works of art directly to social conditions, we should be omitting all reference to psychological factors, and so, by implication, asserting these factors to be of no relevance to the understanding of art.(18)

The coming together of art history and the psychologies of perception has been highlighted in the past generation in the work of Rudolf Arnheim and Ernst Gombrich. Anxious to end what he termed the 'academic gang warfare' that has bedevilled the methodology of art history, Gombrich has pointed out that 'Art versus History is No Contest', and emphasised that

I cannot quite envisage how art or the arts can ever clash with History. History is everything that has been done and as soon as works of art or pieces of furniture are made they are part of history.(19)

Many history teachers who have embraced the 'new history' would find common ground with Gombrich when he compares the study of the history of art with the re-assembly of a jigsaw, a process which demands a high degree of perception and the linking of superficially unrelated clues

There is no practical or theoretical limit to the evidence that may help us in our historical detective work any more than there is in forensic science.(20)

There are other, more profound reasons why the history teacher interested in the visual dimension should consider the work of Gombrich, particularly in the central importance he attaches to 'pattern' for those who create and those who perceive both pictorial representation and decorative art. The pattern or internal representation is the essential image or picture in the mind and reflects the way the brain attempts to sort out what is perceived. In the recent Wrightsman Lectures, Gombrich suggested that

the perceiver possesses and applies to the visual stimuli just the very same schemata (or internal representations) that the pattern maker possessed and employed in producing the pattern: an explanation that is available given only that the pattern maker should have accepted a further constraint - that of visual intelligibility.(21)

The creator or pattern-maker may produce a simple pattern which accords harmoniously with the image in the mind of the perceiver. Gestalt psychologists believe that satisfying art answers a need for harmony, the need to make 'closures'.(22) In contrast, the creator may produce a more complex pattern and may incorporate an inconsistent or 'rogue' element within the constraints of the medium, which prompts questioning. The more complex the visual becomes the more the curiosity of the perceiver is stimulated, always provided the creator has remained within the parameters of the particular medium. However, there appears to be a cut-off point beyond which too much complexity baffles or irritates, so that interest wanes.

Since individuals perceive in different ways, the extent to which the perceiver accepts, questions or rejects is dependent largely on individual expectations. This notion of expectations - centred on the pictures in the mind - is important. In perceptual terms, if expectations are completely or too easily fulfilled nothing new will be discovered; if what is seen is completely different from expectations the pattern of the creator may also have no effect. If however, the image provided by the creator is slightly different from what the perceiver expected, the difference can be coped with and ideas modified. Expectations in this sense have an important function, for the artist can only hope to shock, change, or defy if he is working within certain parameters, which are partly dependent on culture and environment.

If the picture in the mind of the perceiver proves very different from the pattern produced by the creator the results can be dramatic, and one or two examples may be cited. In the *Burial at Ornans,* Courbet painted a group of men and women as they might appear when attending a village funeral and, contrary to the traditional manner, he refused to harmonise the figures - as they actually appeared - into some false, higher meaning. The Paris art public were shocked at the 'reality' which differed markedly from their 'picture in the mind' expectations, and Courbet was accused of vicious exaggeration in revealing a mass solitude in face of the grave.(23) The relationship between an artist and the social and economic milieu in which he works is never easy to define; while the extent to which an artist chooses to please his patrons or himself will vary from one individual to another, so that it is not always possible to accept the maxim that 'we that live to please must please to live'. In 1772 Queen Charlotte commissioned from Zoffany, who was about to go to Italy, a picture of the Grand Duke of Tuscany's Tribuna, which contained a high proportion of the world's most famous pictures and sculptures. As painters of art galleries had often done, Zoffany made a number of alterations in the correct arrangement of what was actually there in order to suit his composition. This kind of artistic licence was not unusual and, in itself, was unlikely to overturn the 'pictures in the mind' against which artist and patron set their expectations. What came as a shock, to the fury of the Queen and George III, was Zoffany's introduction into the picture of a number of Grand Tourists, who were, according to Horace Walpole

> *as impertinent as the names of church wardens stuck up in parishes whenever a country church is repainted and white washed.(24)*

The relationship between patron and artist is often at its closest where personal or family portraiture is concerned. In some instances the creator was able to produce an image which corresponded almost completely with the way in which the patron wished to be seen. Once Van Dyck had shown Charles I his own 'ideal reflection' and had provided a sense of the heroic, the new pattern was extensively copied in a wide range of visual media since contemporaries of the Flemish painter had 'learnt to see with his eyes'.(25) The completion of commissions has rarely provided such mutual satisfaction. According to Sir Walter Raleigh, portraits of Elizabeth I of which she did not approve 'she knockt in pieces and cast into the fire'; while Winston Churchill's dislike of the Graham Sutherland portrait arose largely because it did not meet the expectations of self-image.

> ... *He had come to accept an image of himself, which had become an international symbol; and this Graham had completely disregarded ...(26)*

The identification of visual evidence which differed from the expectations of contemporaries may be of particular significance for the historian. Changes in the way the visual creator viewed the world may reflect fundamental modifications in the way individuals or groups viewed their self-image. Some understanding of how visual forms were received is also important for, if contemporary perceivers experienced pattern-break or 'expectational shock' it is likely that it sparked off questions, inquiry and the search for explanation with which the historian may attempt to empathise. The questions of contemporaries and latter-day historians - the former directly experiencing 'expectational shock' and the latter rediscovering it - may not be dissimilar. Why did the visual creator choose to produce his work in a particular form? Was it accident or design? What personal or social factors influenced the artist? Were the changing elements reflected in the visual a manifestation of contemporary changes in the physical world or mental environment? The historian looks for evidence that will help in the reconstruction of the social setting of the arts in a given age and the quality of a period's response both to the real world and to art. The historian's task is to describe the imaginative as well as the material nature of the past and to essay the possible connections between the two.

IMPLICATIONS OF THE RATIONALE

The implications of accepting the rationale outlined above are considerable, and can only be effected if historians are prepared to consider a wide range of visual material and other sources, so that, through experience and record linkage, a position is reached whereby there is some understanding of 'perceptual expectation'. In simple terms, it means being able to identify particular visual forms; to ascribe them to a particular period or culture; and through continual questioning, to have some awareness of the function, problems and possibilities of such forms.

The rationale can be used in looking at periods of great change, for example, the period of the Italian Renaissance and the Industrial Revolution in Britain. How far can a study of visual evidence reveal both changes in the physical world and mental environment and also attitudes to change itself? In *The Art of the Italian Renaissance*, published more than seventy years ago, H. Wölfflin continually asked himself the questions: what was in the minds of the great Renaissance painters and sculptors when they conceived and executed pictures or statues; and how did the problems of art, and the ways of solving them, present themselves to each in turn?(27) Selecting certain religious themes commonly depicted in the fifteenth and sixteenth centuries, the different ways of treating certain features could be demonstrated by comparing the compositions of Raphael and his peers and the like features in their predecessors, a technique brought out by the juxtaposition of photographs of particular works of art. More recently, Gombrich in *Norm and Form* (1966) considered the origins and growth of the Renaissance idea of progress made familiar by Vasari in his *Lives*, and demonstrated that the concept of artistic progress itself helped to create a climate of ideas which in turn shaped the artists who were exposed to it. For example Ghiberti, while perhaps influenced by classical parallels, was also one of the first of a long line of Renaissance artists to demonstrate in his own work his acceptance of the idea of artistic progress. Along the same line of conscious development, Leonardo attempted to solve his problems of artistic composition in an entirely individual way, and elevated the rapid sketch into an important reflection of the evolving creative process. To some extent, Leonardo went so far beyond the parameters of expectation that some of his ideas were too revolutionary to be generally influential at the time, although his concern with the right artistic solution in composition, rather than with the standard of execution, is a more readily acceptable notion today.(28) The artist of the Renaissance was grappling not only with the subtleties of the visible but was also likely to be as inquisitive as any scientist about how the world actually worked.(29) Thus the historian of the Renaissance needs to have some understanding of what men felt when they looked at nature, and how far their response was conditioned by a sense of beauty, or by circumstance. In providing images of how people saw themselves - and wished to be seen - the artist may also reveal how they felt about the communities in which they lived. The historian wants to be able to imagine how people lived and to consider what possessions reveal about their owners - particularly in societies where art may be a measure of wealth, a store of value, and a significant element in commodity production. The historian wants to know about everyday necessities - furniture and clothes for example - how much they cost, how they were produced and how much discrimination was involved in choosing them. He may also want to know the criteria which underlay the choice of luxuries - jewellery, ceramics, glass, cosmetics, wall hangings - and how useful they are as indicators of wealth, status, class or education. For example in looking at the part that taste played in the lives of the Medici and at how and why it changed, it can be argued that the Golden Age became true for Florence because enough people, including perhaps Lorenzo himself, believed in it.

Art, science and industry had close links during the period of rapid economic and social change in Britain in the eighteenth and nineteenth centuries. A study of contemporary art can provide an insight into the nature and timing of industrial and agrarian change; the varieties of regional development; and can reveal something of the attitudes of those who accepted or abhorred industrialisation. When originally published in 1947, F.D. Klingender's *Art and the Industrial Revolution* brought the approach of a social scientist to one of the most fertile periods of British art, describing the alliance between art and science during the process of industrialisation and looking at a period ranging from Newcomen's first engine for raising water (c.1710) to the mid-nineteenth century. Klingender described how individual artists depicted the visual phenomena of industrialisation which they saw springing up around them - open-cast mining, the arcadian-sited forges and factories of the west and east Midlands, the new canals, and the later railway network.(30) The close links between art and the new forces of change can be seen most optimistically in the work of Joseph Wright of Derby, whose choice of candle-lit scientific demonstrations like *The Orrery* and *The Air Pump,* and industrial subjects such as forges and cotton mills broke fresh ground, developing a new mode of sensibility and a new language of pictorial expression.(31) The ferment of interest in scientific experiment and mechanics, especially among the well-to-do middle classes and successful industrialists, was manifested less in London than in the provinces where philosophical societies sprang up, most notably the Lunar Society of Birmingham, many of whose members were friends or patrons of Wright. Similar activities developed in Derby, where Wright's interests were engaged both personally and professionally, while the east Midlands county was one of the cradles of early industrialism. The decision to use water power when Cromford cotton mills were built was one of the turning points in the history of the factory system. Wright painted a number of views of Cromford and was patronised by both Richard Arkwright and Jedediah Strutt, whose portrait he painted.

Wright's images of awakening industrialism contrasted markedly with the history paintings of the eighteenth century, and the new genre of industrial and scientific paintings mirrored both the changes in the physical environment and the enlarged expectations of a new class of patrons. For a man of Wright's background, nascent industrialism represented hope for the future, and he was able to provide entrepreneurs like Arkwright, Strutt and Wedgwood with images of themselves and their industrial creations as they wanted to be seen. The euphoria of Wright was short-lived and, in the succeeding age which perhaps saw the worst excesses of labour exploitation and the rape of the landscape, Blake was to identify industrialism with Satan; a change in mood and attitude which can also be seen in the poetry and prose of the time, the couplets of Erasmus Darwin praising the wonders of science contrasting with the gloomy picture of industrial expansion described by Wordsworth in *The Excursion*. In the early nineteenth century, Turner seems to have been one of the few major artists who could take the manifestations of the industrial age in his stride, showing both factories and the natural landscape in a view of Newcastle-on-Tyne (1823); while twenty years later his enthusiasm for the new railways was expressed in *Rain, Steam and Speed*.

In looking at the onset of industrialisation and agrarian change some attention needs to be given to the depiction of labour. For example, in Joseph Wright's *The Blacksmith's Shop* it seems that everything has been posed and statically arranged and illuminated for the eye of the perceiver. A generation later, in the backwardness of nineteenth-century Spain, Goya produced a very different image in *The Forge* (c.1815-20), which seems to have been painted from the point of view of the workers whom it depicts and where nothing appears to have been posed or revealed for the benefit of the perceiver. It has been argued that this break in visual expectations represents a 'moment of becoming', as one of the few occasions in which workers were depicted in a new way, constituting the eruption of the labouring classes, as a subject, into European painting.(32)

The English landscape painters of the eighteenth century provided the landed interest with images of rural society as they wished or expected it to be, the 'pastoral' picture in the mind which provided a harmonious view of the natural and social order. Traditionally, these composed images of harmony seem to have met the expectations of general historians and art historians alike. Recent scholarship however has suggested the need to reconsider some of these works, particularly those of George Morland in the 1790s at a time when paternalism and deference, which had hitherto determined the relationships within rural society, were threatened with undercurrents of 'sedition' even in the countryside.(33) Application of the 'rationale for looking' suggested above is pertinent. There are dangers in looking at landscapes and seeing what we expect to see, without giving sufficient attention to the way in which particular works were received by contemporaries. If visual images shocked because they did not accord with perceptual expectations, it is important for the historian to examine the nature of the pattern-break and its possible implications. Thus today much of Morland's work is regarded as sentimental and idealised, but some of his paintings were felt, by his contemporaries, to be threatening. For example, in *The Alehouse Door* (1792) two labourers regard each other intently as if in serious conversation. Like the figures later depicted by Goya in *The Forge* the labourers look away from the viewer and inward to each other - they are there for themselves and not for the perceiver. Morland, who turned his back on the landed classes, and who seems to have preferred the company of the alehouse, fishermen and smugglers, was not depicting figures of rebellion, but the absence of deference or sentimental appeal excluded the paternalist and the reformer. In the harsh economic climate of the 1790s, the traditional pastoral genre allowed the labourer a degree of autonomy which now seemed a threat to deference. The 'picture in the mind' of the paternalist was changing and it was expected that the artist would mirror that change. By continuing in a manner which did not depict more invigilation and control, Morland's *The Alehouse Door* did not meet the new expectations of the landed classes. In providing a detailed study of *The Dark Side of the Landscape* (1979), John Farrell has assisted the historian in looking at one form of genre painting with new eyes.

THE DEVELOPMENTAL STAGES OF CHILDREN

The detailed study of a variety of visual evidence for a particular period or topic, for example the Renaissance or 'art and the Industrial Revolution' is unlikely to find a place in school below sixth-form level. The use of visuals can be frustrated if insufficient attention is paid to developmental stages in children, and some appreciation is needed of the role illustrations play from the early years of childhood and schooling. Although research into the ways in which children react to illustrations has grown in recent years, there is still much that is not understood by educators and publishers about what certain age or development groups can cope with; while the association of visuals with particular personality experiences or accompanying material make generalisations difficult.(34) Nevertheless, if both graphic expression and visual perception are considered, it seems that children invariably go through a number of development stages.

UP TO ABOUT SEVEN YEARS OF AGE The incentive to draw appears to be largely movement, proceeding from wavy to circular scribble, followed by a variety of simple lines and forms until formalised drawing, generally of the human figure, is reached.(35) This development from dot and line to human form and early pictorialism is common to children's drawings throughout the world; while it has been shown that a child's abstract and early pictorial motifs exist in both prehistoric and indigenous art, which strongly suggests that they are manifestations of normal human response to the stimuli of the visual environment.(36) After the age of five comes more detail, more control of line, and simple backgrounds to figures, although the child is still more concerned to make a kind of diagram of what is known to be there rather than to represent what is actually seen. Some attempt has been made to compare children's drawings with the highly accomplished folk art that has survived from primitive times, but there are difficulties in comparing the mental background of the Stone Age and that of the modern child. On the other hand, there are shortcomings in interpreting archaic art almost wholly in terms of sexual or religious meanings rather than concern for aesthetic compositions.

Research on the use of pictures suggests that children's attention tends to be caught first by details which are of immediate interest. By around three years of age, children have the capacity to pick out and name recognisable objects in pictures, more easily if the illustrations are of complete objects standing on their own. Preference for less complex visual patterns tends to persist at least until 5-6 years of age, and children may find flat, two-dimensional pictures with strong contour lines and little overlapping detail easier to understand. It is probably inappropriate to write of 'history' teaching in the first years of formal schooling, although it is likely that in attempting to develop the young child's awareness of the meaning of 'long, long ago' and 'once upon a time', illustrations or simple artist's reconstructions of the past may play a part. As a result of his work in Dudley, John West suggested that

> *recent practice by inspired and skilful infant teachers should persuade us that even seven years of age is unnecessarily late to begin to develop young children's awareness of the meaning of 'long, long ago' and 'once upon a time'.(37)*

SEVEN YEARS TO ABOUT ELEVEN YEARS After seven years of age most children start to develop better strategies for the presentation and perception of visual material. Partly as the result of being taught, attempts at perspective, proportion and movement improve together with orientation or placing; although not until nine years of age or later do most children stop drawing diagrams of what they 'know to be there', and start grappling with the problems of representing what they 'see'. Gombrich has shown how an eleven-year-old's copy of Constable's *Wivenhoe Park* is really a tidy enumeration of the principal items of the picture, particularly those that would interest a child. Such activity combines both creativity and the development of visual perception skills, for example scanning, searching, discrimination of detail, recognition and use of perspective, fixating, using cues such as relative distance, and matching. By this age, eleven years, pupils may be expected to make a range of representations with a variety of basic media - for example, pencil, pastel, brushes, sponges - and according to given criteria; while in painting, colour-mixing, matching and overpainting (the laying on of coats of opaque colour) will have developed. Representations will be possible from real objects or photographs of objects; from given verbal descriptions; or from memory. Again, through line-drawings, pupils may indicate their awareness of pattern and structure in both the natural and the man-made world. According to given criteria, for example tone or scale, pupils should be able to place objects from supplied cut-outs into a given background, thus indicating a growing sensitivity to relationships. Three-dimensional awareness will also be apparent and pupils should be able to use a wide range of material - card, paper, balsa-wood, wire, clay - to make simple constructions and models according to well-defined criteria. Inventiveness and the ability to embellish accidentally-formed shapes may also be marked, as will pattern emphasis.

How far can the visual evidence of history be used to foster the development of the creative skills and abilities outlined above? Observation, interpretation, and pattern recognition can be fostered through a variety of 'scissors and paste' activities. For example, in the early 1970s a number of activity booklets were produced for the 8-11 age group, which involved the cutting out and pasting in of some thirty drawings in their correct places on partly drawn backgrounds - many of them historical settings.(38) Other novel booklets provided a centre spread panorama to be filled with Letraset dry print rubdown pictures. The successful completion of a court scene or a battlefield can be enjoyed at many levels and entails a high degree of picture interpretation.(39) Such activity at concrete level involves certain skills which history teachers will be encouraging pupils to practise mentally later on. The colouring of simple cyclostyled sheets of armorials can form part of a study of heraldry for primary school children, while many step-by-step guides to model-making have been published in recent years.(40)

Visits to museums, monasteries, castles, industrial or archaeological sites can arouse the imagination and spark off a range of drawing, painting and other recording activities. Rewarding work by a class of primary school children has been described using medieval brass rubbings with a 'day-in-the-life-of' approach in an attempt to recreate the lives of contemporary men and women. The brasses provided the basis for a range of activities - illustrations, models, the reproduction of a rubbing in silver foil and the production of a 'medieval' illuminated letter.(41) Work is also possible using tombstone rubbings, for graveyards can be a valuable source of information - with biographical details such as the deceased's habitat, trade, manner of death - and the monuments reflecting the British class system.(42)

That younger children's potential should not be underestimated can also be demonstrated by recent projects initiated at the National Portrait Gallery, whose education department aims at helping schools to use portraits to encourage visual literacy, and is able to demonstrate how primary school children can cope with the portrait as a resource.(43) The first departmental exhibition of the National Army Museum included some vivid paintings by London primary school children reconstructing battle scenes of the Crimean War; while an ICA exhibition drew on the talents of children from Belfast and provided a psychological insight into juvenile images of war.(44)

In addition to drawing and painting from verbal descriptions and historical illustrations, children at quite an early age may be engaged in recording and replicating in a variety of ways: collage, silhouettes, tracings and model-making providing just a few examples. Teachers in the humanities at the primary or middle school can rightly claim that in using visual materials from history they are endeavouring to foster aesthetic and physical skills and to contribute to the social and personal development of pupils.

In perceptual terms, preference for more realism in illustration does not generally show itself much before seven years of age and, despite growing perceptual sophistication, it seems that two or three more years may elapse before children will be able to draw more complex inferences - for example what has probably just happened before or is likely to happen in the near future. Research into the question of 'what gives a picture pupil appeal', using a range of illustrations of one type, some drawn from historical sources, suggests that children towards the end of their primary school years tend to prefer visuals which are more complex than they themselves can produce, but that to capture their imagination the picture has to make a clear statement and be intrinsically interesting as well as complex.(45) In general terms, illustrations with colour, realism and activity are known to score highly with primary school children. In *How Things Began,* Mary McNeil used the strip cartoon approach to deal with the development of such themes as writing, clocks and ships, and emphasised details significant for children on each double-page spread. Yet, as Martin Booth pointed out, this is much more than just an attractive and colourful book for non- or early-readers, for the approach employed could help to lay the foundation of historical understanding through the creation of what Vygotsky called 'pseudo-concepts' - the essential prerequisite for concept formation. Such visual images - perhaps crude to adult eyes - could stimulate the young child's imagination and help in the creation of thought patterns, which could be the starting point for more advanced historical thinking.(46)

Examples of simple observation, identification, classification and pattern formation work can often be found in both the school and leisure reading material of young children - activities involving the location of hidden numbers, letters or objects in illustrations; or in the use of a range of pictures which children are asked to group into patterns on the basis of common features or to spot the illustration that does not fit. The recognition of breaks within patterns or 'misfits' can lead to the asking of questions and simple hypothesis construction. Other visual and graphic techniques may encourage simple observation or provide prompters for a language of looking. For example, portions of photographs or other illustrations can be provided, inviting children to guess at the whole; cut-through books can assist in matching or provide imaginative stimuli for the creation of bizarre forms; and the reading of complex illustrations can be assisted by the inclusion of numbered line-drawing keys which assist identification and the naming of parts. From the time when children begin to represent what they 'see' rather than what they 'know' to be there, the naming of parts and cut-away diagrams will play a more significant role. The need for detail 'for the imagination to play on' was recognised in the Plowden Report, although it is regrettable that too many children's books are still published in which the captions do not draw sufficient attention to details. Contemporary illustrations in history can be more misleading than those by modern artists, particularly when they are taken out of their natural context. In the absence of careful captioning, the perceiver may have no idea of identification, dating or attribution, or whether it was supposed to be fact or fiction. It may also be helpful to suggest or explain some of the technical limitations imposed on artists at different periods in history. For example, in *The Book of Art* (1979), which is designed for the 9-15 years age range, the approaches of different artists to the same subject are illustrated to show how they have used different and individual ways, so that the carefully chosen images and accompanying text should encourage children to re-examine ways of seeing.(47)

History is a particularly rich 'house' for the young child, and the visual dimension has played an important role in many primary schools over the years. Illustrations of frescoes, mosaics, sculptures, drawings, paintings and tapestries can leave a lasting impression; the conventions for representing perspective, mass and movement can be learned; and the building up of a perceptual and conceptual code can be fostered. Yet it is likely that at this age, the majority of children receive visual impressions of the past in the form of modern line drawings and artists' imaginings and reconstructions. Although purists may still object to such re-creations, it can be argued that children prefer to see things as they originally were rather than as they were discovered. At its best, the reconstruction and the original can be juxtaposed so that the viewer can see something of the visual and documentary evidence upon which the artist has based the modern illustrated transcription. Sometimes the reconstructions have been based on field work. For example, in *Everyday Life in Roman Britain* (1924) the Quennells went to Italy for parallels to help them in their work of pictorial reconstruction because not a single Roman building stood to its full original height in Britain and could only be guessed at. In other instances, C.H.B. Quennell made good use of manuscripts as he sought to reconstruct and explain how castles, monasteries and churches were built and used; while Marjorie Quennell provided drawings of the daily occupations of contemporaries. Although sometimes criticised for textual inaccuracies in the *Everyday Life* books, the line drawings were generally accepted, and one reviewer in 1929 clearly recognised the educational potential of such work.

> *Would that more of the students coming up to the new universities had been brought up on the works of Mr. and Mrs. Quennell.(48)*

In recent years there has been some refinement of reconstruction, for example in the work of Alan Sorrell; while there has developed a growing tendency to set reconstructions alongside photographs and contemporary illustrations.(49) In *The Castle Story* (1978) the unusual method is used of superimposing line drawings of people, original walls and labels on to photographs of ruins, which with the associated plans and diagrams provide a useful addition to the history of castle building.(50) In *Castles* (1978) an interesting style has been adopted for the perspective of the line-drawings, people and animals have been introduced to suggest scale, and one of the castle ground-plans is indicated by the subtle arrangements of grass tufts.(51) The reconstruction from an original illustration may not be confined to two- or three-dimensional representation. For example, work is possible in dramatic reconstruction from an historical visual. In one instance, pupils dramatised the activity depicted in a visual showing slavery in ancient Rome, and dialogues were recorded.(52)

But is it history? It has been pointed out that

> *the two elements in successful school history - the pupil's dialogue with the past and his mastery of skills of research and publication - both demand study in depth.(53)*

It has also been argued that

> *in order to understand, the child should investigate the process by which the historian achieves his explanation. The concrete evidence which is available to the historian should be made available to the child.(54)*

In his work in Dudley with children aged 6 to 10+ years, West has demonstrated the important role of the visual dimension, story and museum artefact in developing the concepts of evidence, authenticity, age and the ideas of sequence, difference and change. The sequencing of idea pictures is discussed by the pupils, sometimes in the absence of the teacher, in terms of 'earlier and later' or 'before and after'. While not thinking specifically of 'pattern break', it has also been found that there are advantages in children encountering the unexpected

> *The air of mystery, of a puzzle to be solved, a message to be decoded, has produced an unexpectedly high level of close observation and deduction.(55)*

At the same time it cannot be emphasised too strongly that the analytical and critical perception of the visual evidence of history should be accompanied by the recording, transcription and reconstruction of history, often in illustrated or graphic form, besides the more obvious written explanations.

A PHOTOGRAPHIC STUDY OF THE LOCALITY

By the final year of the primary school or the first years of secondary school, pupils ought to have developed the ability to recognise different media, for example three-dimensional artefacts, photographs, paintings, engravings, drawings and printed or woven textiles. Nomenclature of different features of particular media - for example the names of parts of buildings, paintings, and other man-made objects - will be developing, together with the ability to recognise the characteristics of basic forms and sensitivity to differences of shape, texture, colour, tone and style.

By 1977 more than sixty per cent of British households held cameras and there are benefits in 'young historians' gaining practical experience of photography

> *The knowledge of photography is just as important as that of the alphabet. The illiterate of the future will be the person ignorant of the use of the camera as well as of the pen.(56)*

The camera is the new *lingua franca* for worldwide communication, the primary visual force in life, the third eye of everyman and the true folk-art of the modern age.(57) Even at a time of financial stringency, it is likely that a growing proportion of pupils at top primary/early secondary school level will have direct personal access to a camera. Many schools already engage in local projects or integrated study courses which involve an examination of the school area. The use of photography in the study of school and home community has an advantage in that pupils commence from a position of relative experience and are directly affected by environmental changes

> *There is no better way of linking school to the outside world than through photography.(58)*

If it is accepted that 'the city is one huge visual device which we have to learn to read correctly', then street work, town trails and pupil perambulations can be enhanced by the use of photography. Encouraging 'topic groups' or 'district groups' to see themselves as 'reporters' recording 'Our Town' or 'Our Village' has attractive pedagogical possibilities and should help to foster the ability to see likely photographs. The notion of the photograph as a 'document' can be stressed, as can the importance of recording that which is 'now' but will inevitably become part of 'history'.(59) Given time, there are benefits in reporter groups having the opportunity to plan a series of photographs as evidence for a particular theme following a preliminary observation perambulation. One group might choose to show 'A Day in the Life of Our Town'; while others adopted a 'good news' or 'bad news' approach - for example as visitors might see the community in contrast to the places which tourists do not usually see - or a focus on different aspects of community history. In the course of making a photographic record, it is hoped that pupils would begin to acquire both a simple knowledge of the basic principles of the media and become aware of a rationale for looking. For those with some experience, visual awareness can be heightened by experimenting with composition;

> *better photography comes through practice at observing the world and making visual statements.(60)*

Skills can also be developed which are important for the study of history: observation, selection, and pattern formation, so that the photographic record provides the maximum evidence - always given the constraints of numbers of prints - which can be extracted from the theme. Having thought out what the photographs are intended to show, pupils may soon recognise how different camera angles or focus may provide differences in the statement it makes and the impression it conveys. Other members of the reporter group can keep a record of what has been recorded, when and where, which represents other features of the rationale for looking.

Once a local study is under way, attention can be given to how the work will be presented or communicated. With a view to booklet or wall presentation (or slide-tape programme) the reporter groups can assemble a wide range of material - photographs, drawings, paintings, collages, maps, plans, postcards, travel brochures or town guides. Continuing the approach of 'learning by doing', reporter groups can be transformed into editorial 'workshop' groups. There are advantages in suggesting spatial limits on the final presented form as this will sharpen the important notion of editing. In talking through problems of pictorial and editorial coherence discussion may centre on the criteria to be used for final selection, and how illustrations can be juxtaposed in patterns and arranged with the associated written material to fit their 'view' of the community as the 'truth'. Comparisons may be drawn with the newspaper situation to show that the professional photographer rarely writes the caption and never the headline. It can be demonstrated that a photograph by itself may be very limited in its power of analysis. In devising simple captions and graphics to bring out more in photographs and visuals, pupils are gaining direct experience of the rationale for looking, by directing the attention of the viewer to points to be emphasised. Labelling techniques can be fostered, and in more advanced work accompanying explanatory sketches and cutaways may be encouraged. Precision in scale is also important,and it can be shown that the human figure or any familiar object can serve as a yardstick. Other devices can also be employed: directional arrows; 'x' marks the spot; simple side silhouettes of groups of people or buildings, with number inserts and a key; and the inclusion of maps and plans to show the location of topographical photographs.

Without getting involved in complex media technology, pupils can be encouraged to experiment with their presentation and visual arrangements, to suggest or stimulate ideas. For example, it can be shown that 'cropping', that is removing a strip from any of the sides of a photograph, can be used to improve or enlarge key images, and that aesthetic considerations are often regarded by newspaper editors as being as important as evidential ones. Although overriding any considerations of art in photo-journalism is the obligation to the truth, it can be shown that cropping of photographs can be used by the unscrupulous to manipulate the truth.(61) The conscious juxtaposing, coupling or grouping of illustrations can be used to create a variety of moods, including derision or humour. In comparing colour with black and white prints, pupils can consider whether it is possible to get closer to reality with colour, or whether - because of the 'reality' - black and white may be preferable in some instances. In collating illustrations, including maps and plans, attention will probably focus on providing visual patterns that will meet the anticipated expectations of the perceiver, although it may be suggested that if examples are provided which do not fit expectations it will prompt questioning on the part of the perceiver. It may be tempting to exclude certain visuals as giving what may be considered too distorted a view of 'Our Town', but their inclusion can sometimes be justified if they are specifically intended to make the perceiver think.

The introduction of a number of maps or aerial photographs will also open the way for pattern analysis of settlement. Once again the recognition of differences within patterns can prompt inquiry.

> *There are aspects of the pattern of larger settlements, not least its relationship to other patterns, which may be worthy of attention, and if the map is seen here as a source of questions rather than a basis for answers much of interest may usefully be found.(62)*

In preparing and presenting evidence for the local study it may become apparent that there are differences in the media forms. In the case of drawings or paintings, discussion may centre on the extent of artistic licence to be permitted. It can also be pointed out that such media - unlike the split-second photograph - may take several hours or even days to complete and will have, in consequence, a temporal or time dimension within them. If a postcard or photograph showing part of 'Our Town' from a generation or more ago is available, it will be appropriate to take a modern one from a similar camera angle to show 'Then and Now', which may give a very clear meaning to concepts of continuity and change and through which the rationale for looking at visual evidence in history can be examined.

The 'then and now' use of photographs has been employed in a number of published town studies, and, if two or three photographs of different periods of the same district or street are available, the rationale can be followed through.(63) A first stage may be to ask pupils to identify the media, recognising not just that these are 'pictures' of a street scene but that they are photographs taken at different points of time. Pupils can then suggest which photograph shows the earlier scene and list the evidence on which their choice is based. In dating the evidence, many pupils in the early secondary school years will already be able to approximate, an activity which can be facilitated by providing a list of alternative dates from which pupils can select. By asking pupils to speculate about why and how the photographs were taken and the possible identity of the photographer, ideas about attribution can emerge. Having completed initial attempts at the processes of identification, classification, dating, attribution and sequencing, it is possible to demonstrate - through observation and interpretation - that change and continuity are decisive historical concepts. In some respects the visual can prove more rewarding than the written source. Whereas the latter often emphasises change, and may suggest causal factors or consequential implications, the former source may also show what has altered less dramatically or even seems to have remained unchanged. Thus similarities in photographs from different periods (continuity) as well as differences (change) can be noted, assisted by peer group discussion, and possibly prompted by a reconstruction grid. At this stage in the rationale an opportunity can be given for pupils to list the questions they would like to ask about the photographs. The ability to frame questions about aspects of change and continuity is an important feature of history. Questions about the how, what, where and why of change are likely to arise, besides an interest in the people responsible, and the likely results of change. However, it is hoped that pupils would not only ask 'Why has the street changed?' or 'Why have the shops been rebuilt?' but also 'Why is the Victorian town hall still there?'

Using the same photographs, the next stage might be to ask pupils for ex-

Aerial photographs provide useful visual evidence for observation and pattern recognition as shown in these two views of a Yorkshire market town: Wetherby

planations of the recorded changes; and it would be worthwhile looking at the numbers of pupils who gave single-cause explanation and those who had begun to develop an awareness of the multi-causal nature of change in history. Having established 'hypotheses' pupils can suggest how they might 'test' their theories, and discuss the different kinds of evidence of sources which might prove useful. They might also be asked at what point they would be satisfied with their explanation; while an exercise in judgement may be to ask pupils whether the changes they had recorded were for the better or worse.

Other pairings or groupings of visuals can be employed in a similar way to guide pupils through a thinking rationale from observation to explanation, which can include skills, concepts and attitudes. Examples which can be used might include two town prospects in engravings at different times in the eighteenth century; a plan of a village before and after enclosure; or two maps of a district - one before and the other after industrialisation. As a footnote to a local project it may be appropriate to ask pupils to speculate about the future visual topography: yesterday and today comparisons can be given a further dimension by envisaging 'tomorrow'.

PHOTOGRAPHIC PORTRAITS AND THE PROJECTION OF PERSONAL IMAGES

In the study of family history, which has grown rapidly in recent years, the visual dimension has always played an important role, often in conjunction with associated documentary and oral history.(64) A series of individual 'private' photographs can be used to assist in the development of the concept of change. For example, a simple exercise may ask pupils to put a selection of photographs of the same person in a time sequence.(65)

From an early age, many pupils will have been made aware of the preparations before a photograph of themselves or their family was taken - most obviously in the aspects of appearance and apparel. The notion that many personal photographs provide an image of how the subject wishes to be seen can be discussed, as may the ways in which school photographs are composed to project a 'collective image', with symbols of academe or sporting trophies brought out for the occasion, and the 'political hierarchy' of the school demonstrated by the juxtaposition of head teacher, senior staff, and arrangement of pupils. It is important for children to recognise that the personal images projected in photographs or portraits, particularly commissioned works, represent the ways in which people wanted to be seen by others and that 'image' and 'reality' might be in sharp contrast.

Published collections of early photographs may vividly demonstrate that preparations prior to camera confrontation are not new, but occurred from the earliest days of the medium. The diaries and photograph album of Arthur Munby, a London barrister and keen photographer, have revealed something of the difficulties in persuading working women to appear 'natural'.(66) Often individual photographs or collections reveal the lengths to which individuals and groups might go to give an impression of status and respectability. For example, in *Victorian and Edwardian Yorkshire from Old Photographs*, a photograph of 'Abram Peel & Bros' shows how difficult it is to distinguish between the two groups of management and employees.(67) On both sides of the Atlantic photographers in the late nineteenth and early twentieth centuries were still imitating painted portraits by dressing up models and posing them in sentimental situations, or trying to obtain painterly effects by blurring the images in the darkroom.

The elaborate preparations for posed photographs are sometimes described in the reminiscences of photographers. For example, when Lord Snowdon was asked to take official pictures of the Royal Family in 1957, he planned photographs based on eighteenth-century romantic paintings. Occasionally, the camera has succeeded in catching a significant historical moment by providing a picture of posed image - as the person or group photographed would like to be seen - inescapably attached to the reality of their economic and social condition. For example, one photograph in *Victorian and Edwardian Yorkshire from Old Photographs* shows a line of slum children stretched across a street, but a close scrutiny destroys the conventional pose, for the eye of the perceiver moves from the carefully brushed hair, bright staring eyes, and an expression of uncertain pride of one of the children, down to the white Eton collar and buttoned jacket before reaching the rolled trousers and bare feet.(68)

Sometimes, the unusual intensity of photographs can provide perceivers with an element of emotional shock by capturing the paradoxical essence of the medium and providing images that seem to permit the transcending of space and time and the imparting of authentic knowledge, while possessing the possibilities of visual deception. For example, the compilation of C. Obolensky, *The Russian Empire: A Portrait in Photographs* shows the rapport which photographers were able to create with their subjects.(69) The value of photographs as historical evidence is enhanced when they can be placed in context with associated eyewitness accounts and accurate attribution. For example, in 1875 a photographer, John Thompson, and a 'sociologist', Adolphe Smith, recorded in words and photographs the impressions of personalities regarded as representative of working-class districts in London. A photograph of a horse-bus driver may be simply evocative; it takes on new meaning when the interviewer revealed that, after driving for forty years he was still paid only the equivalent of 25 new pence for a 14-hour day, with no pension and only the workhouse to look forward to.(70) The combination of word and photograph is important at this period, since the essays at realism were often overwhelmed by the determination of working-class as well as upper-class figures to strike a posture of respectability. Nevertheless, through the photography of every generation and of every country there runs a thread of honest comment.

> *The most important contribution of photography as an art form lies ... in its unique ability to chronicle life.(71)*

PORTRAITS IN THE PRE-PHOTOGRAPHIC AGE

Whereas the photograph may be used by the historian in his search for the self-image of a nation, class or occupational group, the range of the painted portrait in the pre-photographic periods is less comprehensive. Despite their limitation in social coverage, portraits are an important visual source for history research and teaching and their use in school has increased in recent years. What did the people who appear in history book texts look like? What did they wear? Prince Rupert's white plume or the wart on Cromwell's nose may be remembered long after the arguments over the Divine Right of Kings have been forgotten. Whether the sitters are shown 'warts and all' depended to some degree on how the subjects saw themselves and wished to be seen by their contemporaries or posterity, since portraits provide

> *a microcosm of the visual attitudes governing how people wished themselves to be seen.(72)*

Since most people behave and look partly as expected of them by others, the portrait presents particular problems for the perceiver, who must decide whether 'face' or 'mask' is depicted. Gombrich has emphasised the importance of empathy in projecting life and expression into the still image of the portrait and the need to identify ambiguities shown in the arrested face

> *as far as the perception of expression is concerned, our understanding of other people's facial movements comes to us partly from experience of our own.(73)*

Before introducing portraits as a source in history teaching - particularly in the Tudor and Stuart periods - it is appropriate to consult the published work of David Piper and Roy Strong.(74) While stressing the importance of changing social conditions and differing intellectual tendencies that have moulded the art of the English portrait-painter from the late fourteenth century onwards, attention has also been given to the political dimension of portraiture. For example, in the 1530s Henry VIII seems to have grasped the possibilities of self-aggrandisement through the work of a first-class portrait painter, Holbein, who brought to England the full impact of the High Renaissance first to the Humanist group around Sir Thomas More, finally to provide the self-image of an entire stratum of English society. Holbein's work has also been shown as a facet of the political scene when the King was assuming supreme power over the Church. Attention may also be given to the role of the portrait in international affairs, exemplified in Holbein's unfortunate portrait of Anne of Cleves. The self-image of monarchy is also apparent in the reigns of Henry VIII's successors. For example, although there is perhaps no other person whose visual image is better known than Elizabeth I's, there is only one portrait which can be established on a documentary basis as being a direct record of her features. Loving personal display and concerned greatly for her public image, it is impossible to appreciate the portraits of Elizabeth without some understanding of the allegory and symbolism in dress, jewels and visual background, the patterns of which were disseminated through various studios. The monarch with orb and sceptre standing on her Phoenix symbol; the sheathed sword; the olive branch; the pelican in its piety: such symbols make more interesting reading than the unblemished mask of Elizabeth, and can be best understood if linked with contemporary literary images. A similar approach of combining portraits with biographies and contemporary descriptions may be recommended for many periods of history.(75)

From the seventeenth century onwards, other approaches become possible. The number of visual interpretations increased for the higher ranks of society, while the beginning of the modern press encouraged the development of social and political caricature. Although Van Dyck died before the outbreak of the English Civil Wars, the Vandyckian image of Charles I long retained its monopoly and was used in the cult of Charles the Martyr. Thus the rather gaunt and uncouth portraits of the 1640s can be set against the heroic ideal presented by the king's favourite painter; while Van Dyck's courtiers can be contrasted with the down-to-earth portrayal of the embattled Royalists by William Dobson. However, despite an alternative portraiture, the Vandyckian image won the day, and his Duke of Hamilton (executed 1649) afterwards provided the 'body' for a portrait of Cromwell.(76) Thus in adopting a contrasting approach - for example, Charles I and the Royalists as they wanted to be seen set against their portrayal by their opponents - it is more appropriate to use portraiture on the one hand and caricature on the other.

The differences within the patterns of buildings and people in William Hogarth's engraving <u>Gin Lane</u> (1751) may stimulate questioning and the search for meaning.

The patterns of buildings and people in Hogarth's <u>Beer Street</u> (1751) contrast sharply with the companion piece, <u>Gin Lane</u>.

CARICATURES AND CARTOONS

Of the visual sources available to the history teacher, one of the most difficult forms is the caricature and, unless some work is done on iconography, allegory and symbolism, it is doubtful whether their potential can be realised before the upper years of the secondary school.

The origins of the caricature and cartoon can be traced back to the popular imagery of the Middle Ages in the grotesques and fantastic or ribald inventions in stone and wood. In the sixteenth century, Luther used pictorial propaganda on a large scale; while later in the century Dutch print-makers attempted the symbolic representation of contemporary political issues, for example when Elizabeth I was depicted as the goddess Diana confronted by the Papist whore of Babylon.(77) The classical and religious symbolism of the early caricatures, and even of those which appeared during the English constitutional conflicts of the seventeenth century, probably preclude their widespread use in school.

Pictorial social satire is more widely used in the secondary school, perhaps most obviously in the work of Hogarth. It has been argued that 'earthbound realism remained the hallmark of the Hogarth tradition', and courses in social history can help to provide some knowledge of his time without which appreciation of his work is difficult.(78) Yet even where the particular human condition which Hogarth wants to hit at is identified, there are dangers in over-emphasising realism. For example, *Gin Lane*, which is often studied as a statement of the effects of alcoholism on the body politic of a city was, like its companion piece *Beer Street*, first issued in the wake of Fielding's alarmist *Late Increase in Robbers*.(79) *Gin Lane* seems to depict the lives of the lower classes in eighteenth-century London, and it was based on a traditional framework of morality, its moral outrage apparently directed at the alleged 'extravagance' of the poor. If Hogarth pioneered a new visual fidelity to the urban world, he patterned this 'realism' into a traditional morality.(80)

Hogarth's graphic powers may be readily appreciated, but it is also essential to consider the allegorical and iconographical patterns which he employed. The traditional iconography inherited from the Renaissance and Baroque courts of France and Italy had lost much of its expressive power by the early eighteenth century, but, even in the different society of Georgian England, artists could not rid themselves altogether of the older allegorical imagery. In devising a new artistic language to investigate everyday life, Hogarth chose to challenge or mock well-known allegorical patterns.(81) *Gin Lane* is crowded with moral emblems and social and religious allegory, the pictorial schema (internal representation) being drawn from the medieval device of 'antithesis'.(82) For example, madonna and child takes the grotesque form at the forefront of the visual of a mother taking snuff and letting fall her son - and family life, the basis of society, is broken.

The rationale for looking can be followed in a close examination of *Gin Lane*, where two patterns - buildings and people - predominate. Within the pattern of crumbling buildings and dilapidation three properties, the pawnbroker, the distiller and the coffin-maker, stand out as exceptions. These businesses flourish in contrast to the disorder and decay of the other populace of the

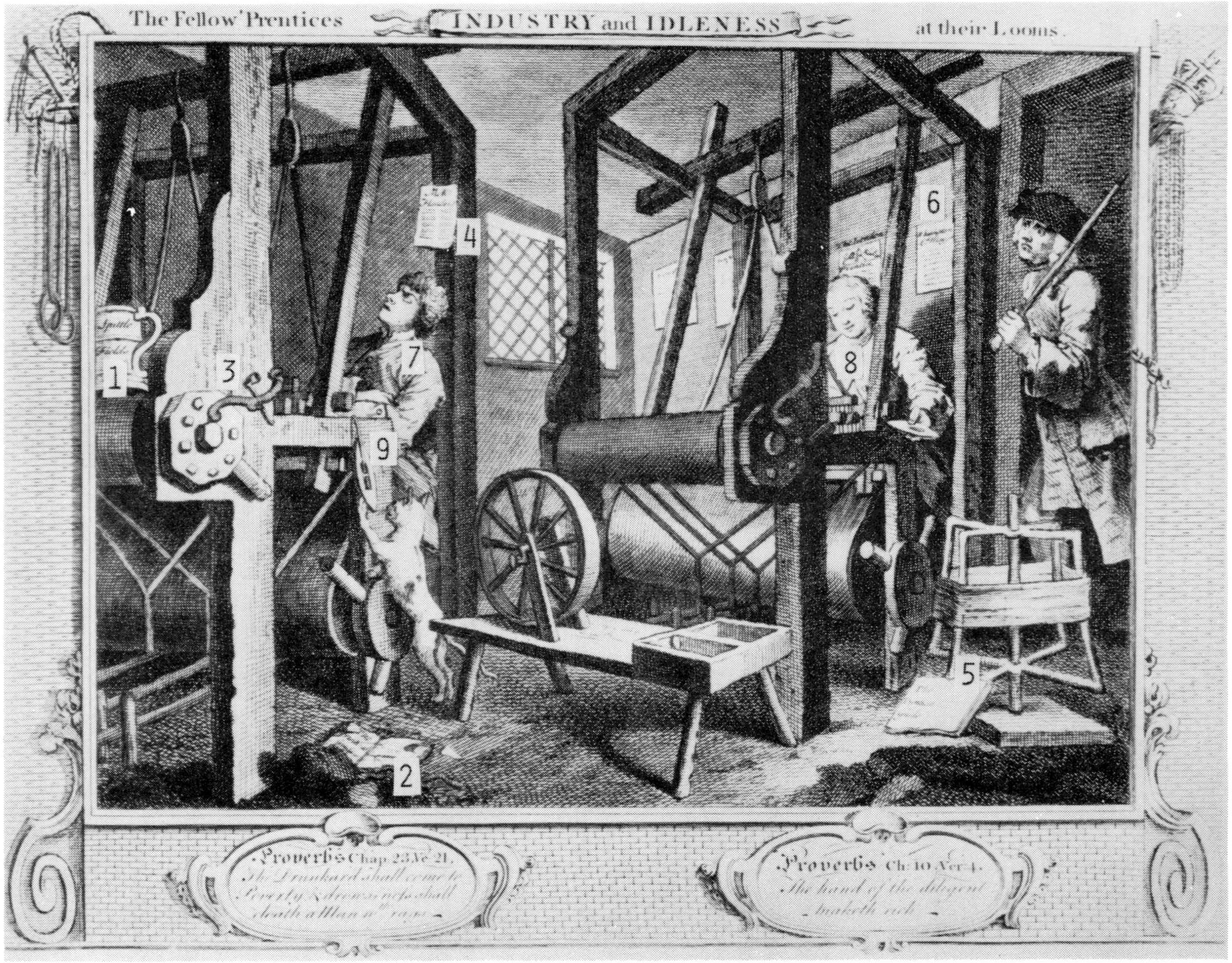

The first of a set of 12 engravings by Hogarth, ***Industry and Idleness*** *(1747). The series illustrates the contrasted careers of two Spitalfields apprentices, Frank Goodchild and Tom Idle. The numbers refer to textual explanations.*

district, the rioting crowds, and the threat of starvation emphasised by a man struggling with a dog for a bone and a near-skeleton gin seller. Having established the breaks in pattern, it is possible to ask a number of questions and to look for explanations. Hogarth provides a range of answers to possible specific questions. For example, if the question is asked, who is the man who has hanged himself? it is possible to deduce that this is the barber, both from the sign and because the inhabitants of *Gin Lane* have ceased to care about their appearance. Or it is possible to ask why certain business activities prospered? and what was the connection between a pawnbroker, a distiller and an undertaker? Altogether, it is possible to list sets of questions relating to decay and disorder; and other questions relating to the apparent prosperity of certain activities. In *Gin Lane*, Hogarth seems to leave the perceiver with a monocausal explanation to both sets of questions.

Similarly, the rationale can be employed in studying *Beer Street*, where drink - based on moderation and British malt - celebrated civic harmony and prosperity. The contrast with *Gin Lane* could scarcely be more marked, and 'spotting the differences' can be centred on the two patterns of buildings and people. In *Beer Street* the properties are all in good repair with the exception of the pawnbroker's, who is in such dire poverty that it is necessary to serve his beer through a grill to prevent the intrusion of unwelcome creditors. Whereas the Chequers Inn is receiving an architectural facelift, the shop sign of the pawnbroker sways unsteadily, the walls are buttressed and a solid mousetrap can be glimpsed through a broken window. The break within the pattern arouses curiosity and invites inquiry: why was the pawnbroker not prospering in *Beer Street?* The answer was suggested by the artist - the people have regular work, they are successful and literate - even the fish girls read a ballad - and have no need of the pawnbroker. Yet to the left of the visual, the sign painter also invites attention as a possible contradiction or 'rogue' element within the pattern of people. Why, when others are shown to be prospering and well fed, was the artist shown to be poor? Was Hogarth here commenting on the position of the artist in society - that even within a prosperous community he found it hard to earn a livelihood?(83)

Because the graphic satire of Hogarth incorporates so many concrete symbols, his work is most appropriate to foster visual literacy at school level and, fortunately, the art historians have provided the necessary guidelines to 'read' the artist who, perhaps more than any other, was responsible for establishing the line of English graphic satire.(84) From an early age, many children have an opportunity to 'spot the difference' and to record, often competitively, slight differences between two illustrations. Using Hogarth's *The Fellow 'Prentices at their Looms* it is possible to devise a picture A and a picture B contrast within a single engraving. For example, on the left of the engraving the idle apprentice is asleep*(7)*, a cat is playing with the shuttle*(9)*, a beer tankard*(1)* and pipe*(3)* are placed close to hand, and 'The Prentice's Guide' at his feet is in a ruinous condition*(2)*. Above his head is pinned the *Ballad of Moll Flanders(4)*. In contrast, on the right the industrious apprentice is busy at the loom*(8)*, there is no pipe or tankard, 'The Prentice's Guide' is well preserved*(5)*, while the *Ballad of Whittington, Lord Mayor* is on the wall behind*(6)*. As if to give more emphasis, two contrasting verses from 'Proverbs' are included. The same engraving also incorporates another feature of Hogarth's series, for example *Rake's Progress, Harlot's Progress* and *Industry and Idleness*, namely, the inclusion of symbolic or iconographic detail which will suggest future developments. At the border of *The Fellow 'Prentices at their Looms* on the side of the idle apprentice is a noose, whereas on the right, the shuttle hand of the industrious apprentice can be followed diagonally to the cane of the master (symbol of discipline) and so to the mace of the Lord Mayor. Having listed the main differences, it is possible to consider how far the engraving reflects the attitudes of the time towards such matters as work, discipline, and crime; and to what extent such views survived into the succeeding industrial age. Leigh Hunt, the nineteenth-century poet and essayist, in recalling his schooldays at Christ's Hospital recorded:

> *The children's books in those days were Hogarth's pictures taken in their most literal acceptation. Every good boy was to ride in his coach, and be a lord mayor; and every bad boy was to be hung, or eaten by lions.(85)*

In the main, social cartoons retained their basic devices of ridicule and satire to the reform of customs, manners and laws in the work of those who followed Hogarth, and in particular Thomas Rowlandson, James Gillray and George Cruikshank.

By the mid-eighteenth century, England was gaining notoriety for the licence of its political and personal satires as Abbé le Blanc recorded:

> *The pleasantries of their pictures are like those of their writings, flat, heavy and overdone; they are a sort of national pleasantries, which divert none but themselves. These political prints, which appear daily against the ministry, are all of this stamp: they have not the least delicacy, and are remarkable only for the grossness of the satire.(86)*

Despite some prosecutions for sedition and obscenity, England was renowned for its toleration, contrasting in many ways to the Ancien Régime across the Channel. Thus in *Tableau de l'Angleterre* (1788) the author looked at the cradle of political satire:

> *Il faut compter au nombre des privilèges de cette nation la liberté de faire des gravures satiriques, qui tournent au ridicule les ennemis du jour. Le Français les chansonne, le Hollandais plus pesant frappe des médailles; l'Anglais a choisi la gravure, comme le plus propre à donner de la publicité à la satire.(87)*

Political cartoons were usually produced to emphasise differences and increase the political temperature, and the period of the French Revolution and Napoleonic Wars provided new scope for the caricaturists. The satirical prints of Gillray and his contemporaries permit a deeper study of the impact of the French Revolution: Charles James Fox becomes a ferocious sans-culotte, Brooks's Club becomes a Jacobin stronghold, and St. James' Palace goes up in flames. In France, the arts acquired a more explicitly political function as attention was directed to supposed enemies of the Revolution. In September 1793 the Committee of Public Safety invited David, one of its deputies

> *to use all the talents and means at his disposal to increase the number of prints and caricatures which will rouse the minds of the people and make them feel how odious and ridiculous are the enemies of Liberty and of the Republic.(88)*

Many French prints were directed against the English, and both nations, in circumstances of mutual suspicion and fear, were depicted by one another in grossly distorted images.

To grasp the point of caricature, historians need to look at the political, social and artistic background and to identify and understand the events that inspired caricaturists to particular forms of symbolic imagery. It is also important to be sensitive to graphic changes in nuance, demonstrated, for example, in recent scholarship on the ways in which the Irish were portrayed in nineteenth century caricature 'from a drunken and relatively harmless peasant into a dangerous ape man'.(89) James Gillray portrayed the Irish peasants of 1798 as brutal and degraded, while a caricature of 1843 represented Daniel O'Connell as having conjured up 'the Irish Frankenstein'. Anti-Irish prejudice can be seen in the illustrations of comic artists like Leech and Tenniel, but perhaps most disturbing is the recent suggestion that Victorian Englishmen, disturbed by Darwinian speculation that men and apes might have evolved from a common ancestor, may have found a degree of psychological relief by representing

> *the Irish and other lesser breeds ... as a buffer or evolutionary cordon sanitaire between themselves and the anthropoid apes.(90)*

What is even more disturbing is that there seems to be some evidence that such attitudes were not uncommon. The first live gorilla arrived at London Zoo in 1860; in the same year - although the association was probably not direct - Charles Kingsley referred to Connemara peasants as 'white chimpanzees'. In 1862 it was implied by one writer in *Punch* that the Irish peasant - 'the Irish Yahoo' - might turn out to be the 'missing link' between man and gorilla. With growing fears of the Fenians in the 1860s, London caricaturists increasingly depicted Irishmen as apes, while for months after the Phoenix Park murders in 1882 the London comic weeklies were filled with cartoons of ape-like monsters with huge mouths and sharp fangs.(91) The changing images of the Irish in nineteenth-century caricature suggest that, perhaps underlying the familiar 'logic' for English rule in Ireland, was a deeply held but irrational conviction that the Irish were by nature incapable of self-government.

Of the various cartoons used in school, the most common are probably those reproduced from *Punch*. Modelled on the Paris *Charivari*, the foundation of *Punch* brought a great change to English comic art, and transferred the caricature from the street to the home. Sometimes the social cartoons require little explanation and can be used for 'spot the difference' activities: for example, one *Punch* cartoon, 16 March 1910, which shows a scene in 1900 with a cart horse towing a broken-down car, and a scene ten years on with a car towing an early bi-tri-plane, a simple 'then and now' purporting to show how the private car had become a more reliable form of transport for the wealthy classes.(92) Similarly, a 1911 cartoon, 'A Decade's Progress', summed up the transformation in women's fashion.(93) Occasionally a *Punch* cartoon attempted to predict the future, and the graphic point is recognisable in today's world, for example the Martian appearance of batsmen facing fast bowlers in 1854.(94) However, humour does not always travel so well or so immediately from one age to another, and many of the cartoons which comment upon the contemporary scene may lose some of their comic impact. If access is possible to a long time-span of *Punch* volumes, the transformation of the periodical from a champion of the 'underdog' in the 1840s into a mellow, middle-class family periodical of the 1890s can be demonstrated, reflecting at the same time the transformation in class attitudes in Victorian England.

Political cartoons can tell the historian whether certain scandals were public knowledge, or which groups tried to manipulate public opinion. They offer contemporary interpretations of events and can provide insights into the popular attitudes that underlay public opinion. However, the heavily symbolic cartoons of statesmen and personified nations do not always make straightforward 'reading' and may well necessitate the inclusion of a glossary. Another approach is to use a number of cartoons for a short period, for example 1853-54, and to highlight one issue, for example the background to the Crimean War, so that a glossary can quickly permit pupils to recognise the contemporary political animals: the lion (Great Britain), the bear (Russia), the Gallic cock (France) or the turkey (Ottoman Empire-Turkey). When a package of 12 cartoons was used with sixth-form students to consider 'Some Aspects of 1903', the reaction was very favourable.(95) Cartoons have been used by some public examination Boards, and their use can help in teaching the skills of analyzing historical evidence, especially for the nineteenth and twentieth centuries.(96) Despite the problems of bias and propaganda, it is sometimes revealing to see the different ways in which cartoonists portrayed political figures at different times of their careers. For example, *Punch* cartoons of Hitler in 1940 are strikingly different from those of 1945 and reveal much about the changing view held by the British people of the dictator's declining fortunes.

TIME IN A FRAME

By looking at a variety of media it is hoped that children will gradually become aware of what each form can or cannot do. In the pre-photographic period, there were two principal ways of representing events or narrative in a single illustration. For example, in looking at the depiction of a riot or crowd scene it is necessary to consider whether the illustrator intended to show the course of the action, or whether it was designed to sum up the event in a comprehensive panorama. Both conceptions are historical, but the summing-up approach lacks an inner 'temporal' dimension.

If the course of events is the visual theme, the representation will contain more than one moment of time, sequentially and simultaneously portrayed. This technique was used in Froissart's *Chronicles*, showing two significant episodes during the Peasants' Revolt. Within a single visual, the argument between the mayor and Wat Tyler is shown, together with a later moment of time, also at Smithfield, when Richard II appealed to the peasants as their leader. The king and the principal characters appear twice in the same illustration, and the artist used the two-dimensional visual rather like a stage and moved the personalities about. Similarly, in a French miniature painted about 1500 to depict the battle of Roncevaux, Roland is shown in the foreground locked in battle with a Saracen, and also appears in the background blowing his ivory horn. Another contemporary miniature included three views of the Duke of Orleans in the Tower of London, where, after defeat at Agincourt, he spent twenty-five years in prison.

The incorporation of two or more episodes in a single visual is not confined to French miniature painting. The juxtaposition of religious scenes can be seen in a variety of media, a left-right sequence often being adopted in the pre-printing period. For example, in a single fresco picture at Pickering parish church three episodes are shown in the story of John the Baptist, namely, the feast with Salome dancing, St. John being beheaded, and Salome carrying his head on a dish. In this instance, the way the story was depicted probably owes a lot to the form in which it was shown in the streets of York as a mystery play or pageant.(97) Sometimes 'stories' were shown on such media as misericords, most notably at Ely Cathedral, although it has been suggested that contemporary manuscript illustration had some influence on the evolution of the misericord from single motif to expansive narrative.(98) The technique of depicting numerous points of time and place in a single illustration probably reached its height in the sixteenth century as seen in the 'portrait of the life' of Sir Henry Unton (c.1596).

The scope for introducing visual enigmas and conundrums is likely to be very limited at school level, although presenting children with the unexpected is likely to arouse considerable curiosity. In the sixteenth and seventeenth centuries, 'perspective' and 'turning' pictures were not uncommon. Such trick pictures provided different aspects according to the angle from which they were viewed; or presented a distortion when viewed in the normal way but assumed a proper aspect when looked at slantingly. They were often referred to in contemporary dramatic works, as in Shakespeare's *King Richard II:*

> *Like perspectives, which rightly gazed upon*
> *Show nothing but confusion - ey'd awry*
> *Distinguish form.*

A 'turning picture' of Mary Queen of Scots seen from left to right shows the transformation of the Queen's image into a Death's Head. Almost certainly painted after Mary's execution in 1587, the unsympathetic combination of subjects might reasonably be interpreted as a reflection of English attitudes towards an executed enemy.(99)

Single visuals in which the artist or engraver depicted a political event have special problems in relation to bias as well as incorporating a temporal element. In looking at photographs of Roman military sculpture, for example, it is pertinent to ask children to consider whether they think the mason was working for the Roman army? In the case of war, it can be demonstrated that long before the advent of either universal literacy or the mass media, the pictorial record played an important part in conditioning national response. A variety of visual media - broadsheets, cartoons, paintings and prints for example - were employed for propaganda purposes in earlier centuries. Paintings of the eighteenth century tend to focus on a general or admiral in the foreground, pointing heroically to a distant conflict and, although in the nineteenth century there was a change in emphasis towards the common soldier or sailor, it was usually in an attempt to stress heroism.

Advances in printing techniques permitted the comparatively easy reproduction of sketches by 'special' war artists in the illustrated papers from the mid-nineteenth century. The 'special' made mass propaganda more effective and helped to form the Victorians, notions of war and Empire. Comparisons can be made between the work of the 'special' and the work of the war photographer from the mid-1850s; and their different approaches can be considered - the propagandist, the adventurer, the soldier-reporter, the emotion-drained recorder.(100) It can be shown how the Indian Mutiny inspired the first detailed photographic illustrations of human suffering and provided the camera with an important role in formulating a less romantic and less remote image of war, besides inspiring Vincent Brooks's lithograph of the Chamber of Blood at Cawnpore. Teaching topics such as the Eastern Question, Gladstone, or Disraeli's Second Ministry can be given more vivid meaning when it is pointed out that Frederic Villier's horrific engraving of the burning of three wounded Serbian soldiers by the Turks was part of the reason for the outcry of public opinion against Ottoman misrule in the Balkans.(101)

Looking at the war artists' and war photographers' work in the nineteenth and twentieth centuries and during the two World Wars may prompt children to consider the most crucial question in the study of history, to inquire of evidence, 'Is it true?'. For example, it can be pointed out that although Constantine Guys, a 'special' artist for the *Illustrated London News*, brilliantly depicted the Charge of the Light Brigade, he was not averse to using artistic licence, and instructed the engraver to 'resite' a windmill at Sebastopol in a more picturesque position against the horizon.(102) At the same time, it is important to demonstrate to children the risks of being deceived by a single still photograph, and it can be shown that the medium is not as straightforward as it seems and that what at first sight appears to offer indisputable evidence may have been 'staged' for the photographer. For example, from the Korean War the world saw a photograph of an American soldier sharing his last drop of water with a dying peasant, but, as the *Picture Post* photographer subsequently recorded:

I set it up. Everybody was walking past but I had the idea and asked a GI to give an old man some water for the sake of the picture. He said he would if I was quick - and if we used my water ration.(103)

Thus in this instance it can be shown that, although the camera did not lie - since the American <u>did</u> give water to the peasant - it might be considered an accessory to untruth.(104) Having demonstrated the possibility of 'stage directing' photographs, it can be shown that, through the use of composites - a combination of photographs - people can be 'seen' to be present at the same point of time or at the same place when they were not. Whilst explaining the difficulties in fusing a number of images within a single edited frame, highly skilled photographic techniques do not preclude deception.(105) At the same time it can be pointed out that 'stage direction' or composites may pass public scrutiny unchallenged if the resultant frame provides a symbolic 'truth' and meets the visual expectations of perceivers.

Whereas television, however informative or exciting, is ephemeral (although even this is changing with advanced video-technology), the still photograph can provide permanent visual experience and symbols for an age:

The still picture which made the biggest impact in recent years, that of the Saigon police chief shooting his Vietcong prisoner in the head, would have been lost in a television film. It was precisely its 'stillness' - the sense of the moment frozen in time - that made its impact.(106)

'Cropping' illustrations can be used to demonstrate the possibilities of being deceived by a single still photograph as shown in this example from a Leeds United versus *Leicester City football match (1973).*

VISUAL SEQUENCES AND PICTURE STRIPS

It is important for children to develop an understanding of how the news is made and disseminated; and of the technical possibilities and limitations of the various media. By the early years of secondary school many pupils are likely to be familiar with at least some reportage techniques, such as slow motion film and television sequences, different camera angles, graphic overlays and action replays. A discussion about a particular event - for example a football match - may elicit views on the range of modern media, supplemented where possible by the eye-witness reports of those children who may have attended. Comparisons can then be made with historical sources which covered a sequence of events and which were not confined to one 'frame'. There are many examples of the 'picture strip' technique being used to narrate a story or to project religious or secular themes, including Egyptian wall paintings, friezes in Pompeii, the pictographic annals of the Aztecs, Trajan's column, and the Bayeux Tapestry, of which the last named is probably the most widely used single visual source in school history teaching.

The Bayeux Tapestry has been described as a sequence of propagandist images 'cut' in a manner comparable to a film newsreel.(107) The comparison can be carried further if the Tapestry is considered in relation to the problems of capturing time and space and is examined by means of the 'rationale'. Commissioned by William of Normandy's martial brother-in-law, Odo, Bishop of Bayeux, the Tapestry - woollen thread on linen with Latin sub-titles - was probably embroidered by English craftswomen and is likely to have been completed by 1080. It was probably intended for a feudal castle rather than a church, although it has been in the possession of the cathedral at Bayeux since at least 1470.(108) The picture strip is about 49 centimetres wide and 70 metres long, being made up of 72 pictures, with continuous top and lower borders crowded with symbolic and iconographical detail. At school level, scenes from the Tapestry are often used to demonstrate contemporary armour, weapons, ships, horsemanship or castle building; and to show how it depicts events between 1064 and 1066.

The tapestry scenes follow a left to right sequencing. In each 'sequence' the action commences on the left - the earlier point of time - and concludes on the right. However, two scenes are included which do not fit this pattern and are shown in a reverse right to left order. These are usually dismissed as pictorial conundrums which the designer might have considered pictorially advantageous.(109) Seen merely as statements, the two scenes might be regarded as visual curiosities; looked at as 'pattern-break' within a visual document of considerable physical length other possibilities are opened up. It may be that this technique - pattern-break - was consciously employed by those who designed the tapestry in order to focus attention on the events which were considered to be of particular significance.

The story opens with King Edward the Confessor apparently giving instructions to Harold before his journey to France. The events leading up to Harold's departure, the Channel crossing, and his arrest by Count Guy - a ruthless vassal of Duke William of Normandy - all move left to right. The first pattern-break occurs with the arrival of William's messengers - from the right - to demand Harold's release. Following the 'rationale for looking', questions arise and explanations are sought. To highlight the dramatic events, the 'artistic director' of the tapestry sets his audience in a

Left (earlier point of time) - right (later point of time) sequence: King Edward the Confessor sends Earl Harold of Wessex on a mission to Normandy (probably 1064)

Left - right: Harold crosses the English Channel

Harold swears allegiance to Duke William of Normandy

Right - left sequence: The funeral procession of King Edward which is depicted preceding a 'two-in-one' showing Edward sick (top) and being laid in state (lower) 5 January 1066

Left - right: William holds a Council of War

Left - right: the invasion fleet crosses the English Channel

The later stages of the battle, 14 October 1066

The death of Harold. Could this be another 'two-in-one', showing Harold's helmet pierced by an arrow and then hacked down with a sword?

situation which can reveal William, the hero of the propaganda piece, in the best possible light. Why did the messengers seek to release Harold? A speculative answer - that William was an honourable man who, in the best tradition of Roland, was acting out of friendship. The sequences now revert to the left-right pattern and, having cemented their friendship in several military exploits together, Harold is shown swearing loyalty to William over sacred relics as an oath of allegiance. This completed, the scene is set for Harold's return to England.

The second 'visual break' comes about half way through and is made more dramatic by the use of another convention. Two different time scenes are shown in one sequence, which shows Edward the Confessor sick and surrounded by friends; and then the dead king. The significance of the event is further heightened by another right-left sequence showing Edward's funeral procession to Westminster which precedes spatially the two-in-one deathbed sequence. Without the death of Edward there would presumably have been no Norman Conquest at that time, and indeed no tapestry.

Following the break, the second 'half' opens dramatically with Harold being offered, and accepting, the English crown, an act contrary to the oath, and treason to his erstwhile friend William. Norman claims to the English crown lay in the argument that William had been promised the throne by Edward, who had gone so far as to send Harold to Normandy to confirm the promise. Thus betrayed, the propaganda piece can show William deciding to invade England in a just cause. In class, it is hoped that pupils might discuss the 'bias' or 'neutrality' of the tapestry. For example, it can be pointed out that extant Anglo-Saxon sources make little reference to the alleged promise.

Throughout the later stages of the tapestry, the left-right space-time pattern is unbroken, but a question which has often been raised is that of the final fate of Harold. The first mention of Harold being pierced in the eye was made thirty years after the battle and has often been discounted. Could the figure whose helmet had been pierced, and the one to the right - hacked down by a Norman knight - both represent Harold, shown close together at different moments of time? We cannot be sure, but it is worth emphasising that the first 'half' of the tapestry ended with different moments of time encapsulated in a single frame. Could it be that the 'artistic director' used the technique again to complete it? Such speculation depends partly on the assumption that the tapestry is complete, a matter of discussion among historians.

A leading authority on comics maintains that the medium is both work of art and aspect of social history.(110) There have been several histories of comics, many referring back to ancient Egypt, the Bayeux tapestry, and the 'balloon' techniques of Gillray and his contemporaries.

The problem of tracing origins centres partly around the question of definition. If the comic strip is defined as a mass-produced, printed sequence of separate images which tell a story but whose captions must be subordinate to the pictures, then it seems that the genre was invented in fifteenth-century Germany.(111) Such 'sequences' served as political and moral propaganda and reveal something of the habits of people - mainly middle-class - who bought and read them: their acceptance of vicarious violence, their pronounced prejudices, and their interest in current affairs. Hogarth elevated the comic illustration to high art and made it intensely satirical; while it reached a new intensity in Goya's *Caprichos* and *Disasters of War*.(112)

In school, attention may well focus on the landmarks in comic history, particularly in Britain. Initially, the comic was aimed at young working-class adults. Even before the arrival of universal elementary education, the first British strip hero - or rather anti-hero - *Ally Sloper*, a cynical ne'er-do-well, had appeared in *Judy*, a weekly magazine modelled on *Punch*. Probably the first British comic, *Funny Folks* (1874), was intended for adults, as were the other comics of the Victorian period, including *Comic Cuts* (1890). *Puck* (1904) commenced as an adult comic but was finally taken over by its children's section; *Rainbow* (1914) was expressly created for children; and by 1920 there was the hyphen-strewn *Chick's Own* designed to help the very young to read. The surviving comics now largely jettisoned their adult readers, a curious transformation in the genre which merits a place in social history.

The availability of a wide range of comics from different periods might enable a study to be undertaken of changes within the genre. For example, the arrival of new heroes from across the Atlantic from the Second World War onwards finally inspired a new kind of hybrid in Britain, *Eagle*, a modification worth consideration. For many of today's children, the Second World War has assumed a place in mythology as potent as the American West. Some teachers might question the value of introducing war comics - which often glorify violence - into the classroom. Yet children cannot be wholly sheltered from such material, and it is not inappropriate to place war comics in context, to set them alongside other evidence and to discuss them in terms of bias, propaganda, and national stereotypes, as well as considering logistical accuracy. It might prove a salutary lesson to compare war comics of today, for example *Battle*, with those which actually appeared during 1939-45.

> *The war came into regular comics all the time. There were strips about evacuees and air raid wardens and spies and so forth. Sexton Blake was often up against fiendish secret weapons. But little of it was remotely based on fact ...(113)*

Naturally, where a series of illustrations has been used to show political events, problems of bias have to be considered, particularly if the visuals originate from a single source.

In introducing the comic strip into the classroom, the form is as important as the content. History teachers often ask pupils in top primary/early secondary school years to record or present work in picture strip form, which is also widely used in text books. It can be argued that pupils should be encouraged to develop graphic conventions in producing their own comic strips. A variety of captioning and timing techniques can be discussed with pupils, including the conventions used in comics for dialogue, 'thought captions' and even flash-back techniques. Leaving 'balloons' blank so that pupils can fill in their own words to tell their story can illustrate that the understanding of pictures is influenced by the accompanying words. Jules Feiffer, writing about American comic-book artists, described how he and his colleagues strove, through cinematic angling, cutting and close-up, to make their 'heroes' appear to move.(114)

Although comic strip heroes have the propensity to overcome space and time, the serious study of the genre will quickly involve pupils in sequencing, a concept on which growing emphasis has been placed in history teaching in recent years. As a practical exercise, pupils can be presented with comic strip 'frames' which have been purposely distributed out of sequence and are to be re-ordered into a pattern to tell the story. This stage successfully completed, pupils can be asked to turn the picture story into the kind of script that the artist might originally have worked from. That completed, a strip for either the previous or the following week's episode can be designed with appropriate pictures and dialogue 'bubbles', 'thought graphics' or other narrative conventions. Most children read comics uncritically, and an awareness of the techniques of the medium can assist in the development of literate skills.

EVERY PICTURE SELLS A ...

Although it can be demonstrated that advertising is 'as old as humanity' it is unlikely that the earlier forms - for example the 'Cris de Paris' of the Middle Ages or the works of Bruegel which include inn signs and tradesmen's boards - are widely used at school level. However, illustrations of the sign boards of inns or shops of eighteenth-century England can be used to study the pre-industrial age, with pupils being placed in the situation, 'Imagine you woke up in London in 1750 ...'(115) Pupils can also design their own signs, an exercise which is enhanced if supporting information is provided. Attention can also be given to the trade announcements and the techniques or promises of the quack doctors of the period. Although 'then and now' contrasts can be made, it can also be shown that, even at that time, some strikingly up-to-date comments were aired about advertising, most obviously perhaps by Dr. Johnson in the *Idler* (1759):

> *the trade of advertising is now so near to perfection that it is not easy to propose any improvement.*

By the later eighteenth century, the advertising poster had become a prominent visual feature in many European cities. Describing Paris just before the French Revolution, Mercier's views have relevance today:

> *Now posters constitute a course in human morals, politics, and literature ... they form a public library, permanent, full of instruction, a visible record of human acts, plans, and conceptions, however odd and fugitive. At every street corner speaking to you of your health, your fortune, your pleasures, your coming movements, and holding daily converse with you on matters of physique, diplomacy, money matters, or cooking. Thirty-two placards advertising public shows, always in proximity and always in competition, show us a whole populace in the assiduous service of these new temples of idleness, and prove that our pleasure resorts equal the spacious Roman circuses, and that we love sights and toys as much as those ancient masters of the world ... The poster covers, colours, dresses Paris one may say, at the moment when these lines are written (c.1788).(116)*

Pasted-up advertisements, the so-called 'poor man's gallery', proliferated in the nineteenth and early twentieth centuries, largely it seems, unchecked.

> *One poster tells you that you suffer, or soon will suffer, from headache, nausea, giddiness, colic, while its neighbour on your right offers you cocoa for breakfast. On your left hand, snuggling against the cure for colic, another poster - it is gallantly designed - puts you on horseback and hands you a green bottle of venerable whisky-corked. Then you receive a pressing invitation to be a father with many children, all of whom are devoted to a delicious patent food ... After walking a few yards you are asked to visit Tunis, to fill your mouth with toffee, to take a mild purge daily before breakfast, and to choose between two tonics - one supreme and the other the greatest of all restoratives.(117)*

However, regulations for controlling the display of outdoor advertisements were introduced under the Town and Country Planning Act of 1948, and today any revival of the poster hoarding depends on the extent to which it can be fitted into orderly town planning.

Extant examples of old posters can usually be found in libraries or museums, while many have been reprinted in recent years, and can be used for a variety of 'then and now' exercises. While the full range of advertisements for any town can never be gauged, the commercial directories from the late eighteenth century onwards often contain examples which can provide a basis for 'an imaginary visit to a town in the reign of ...'. By providing photocopies of a range of advertisements of the period - means of travel, hotels, newspapers, telegraph, public baths and gardens, shops, photograph or daguerreotype gallery - pupils can be invited to select examples and to state reasons for preferences from a range of alternatives.(118)

Advertising in the twentieth century derives much of its aesthetic from high art, both painting and literature, and what at first sight may appear a startling new advertisement may well derive from classical inspiration and iconography. Although often dismissed as a prostituted art, the rise of the medium is not without interest at secondary school level. In the mid-nineteenth century, the artist still scorned the poster - Millais scarcely saw the popularisation of 'Bubbles' in terms of soap-manufacturer patronage - and the turning-point did not come until the advent of the Japanese print in the 1890s. However, by the 1920s art schools were beginning to smile on the art of the poster, which was drawing on many forms of ancient and modern art: Greek vase-drawings, Chinese paintings on silk, Byzantine mosaics, Japanese prints, English brasses, and the drawings of Daumier were all providing 'comparative sources'.(119) Attempts to link the role of oil-painting in the past and of advertising today have been made through comparisons of imagery, and through the arguably similar relation of these art forms to the idea of possession.(120)

The rationale for looking can be applied to advertisements. The use of accompanying text may assist in the earlier stages of identification, classification, dating, and attribution, and children can be asked to identify 'products' - including entertainment and other amenities - and to observe basic patterns. Connotation, or the search for symbolic meaning, can be aided by some understanding of advertising iconography; while attempts can be made to locate the special 'promise' included in many advertisements to permit a particular brand of 'product' to stand out. Thus it can be shown that in Victorian advertisements no holds were barred where famous personages were concerned - even Queen Victoria travels from Windsor to London and enjoys a 'nice cup of Cadbury's Cocoa' on the Royal Train.(121)

Advertisements combine illustration and written caption; they have developed their own iconography and symbolism; and they relate to the everyday experience of pupils. Whether or not one is prepared to accept McLuhan's view that the agencies 'express for the collective society that which dreams and uncensored behaviour do in individuals', it can be argued that aspects of popular and advertising culture merit serious consideration and that, since advertising figures so prominently in the world around us, the recognition of its impact, influence and varied forms should find a place somewhere in the years of formal education.

PICTURE POSTCARDS: SENDING IMAGES

The picture postcard has a complex heritage as visual manifestations of an instinct to embellish and send images. Some attempts have been made to trace the origins back to illuminated manuscripts, medieval woodcuts, broadsides, elaborate advertisement-cards on which tradesmen could write their bills, the *cartes de visite* circulated by the gentry, and the pictorial letter-heads of fashionable watering-places. Thus it is argued that many of the purposes to which picture postcards have been turned were served in earlier centuries by other media. The emergence of the picture postcard as a distinct visual medium dates only from the 1860s, the outcome of a significant conjunction of factors - changes in reprographic techniques, in postal facilities, in patterns of social structure and in leisure pursuits.(122) Although permitted in the mail from 1870, the offical postcards were a Government monopoly until 1894 when privately produced picture postcards were permitted in Great Britain.(123) The development of the medium went hand in hand with the slow democratisation of English social life.

By the beginning of the twentieth century card collecting was a fashionable craze, and deltiology or cartomania has experienced a considerable revival in recent years. In many respects the postcard is an appropriate 'original document' to introduce into the classroom, providing scope for identification, classification, dating and attribution. Whatever the category of postcard - topographical, topical and commemorative, humour, politics, war - it can be used as a document of social history and art. Postcards of the topography of a community at different times can be used to develop concepts of continuity and change or as part of a local study, with the proviso that picture postcards of places often provided an 'idealised' view. Topical and commemorative cards can enable pupils to recognise the events or personalities which were regarded as noteworthy, whether or not these are now deemed of historical significance - a steam tram-car in Leeds, crowded horse-buses in The Strand, a crashed aeroplane, or Edward VII setting off for a drive, seated as if enthroned and already wearing a Safety Belt. Cards featuring humour, politics or war may provide an insight into contemporary attitudes and biases. If large numbers of cards can be introduced into the classroom, they can provide opportunities for exercises in matching, pattern formation and 'spot the misfit' card.

Postcards should also be considered in totality - visual, stamp, address, date and message to be transcribed - and the point made that the new medium enabled people who might be semi-literate to send visual images - perhaps, in the case of sentimental cards, as they wished others to see them. Postcards prolonged many friendships that might not have been sustained by letter, and the visual had to appeal not only to the buyer but also to the receiver, who might treasure it. In Edwardian England, the postcard took the place of the telephone of today and cost only a half penny. With the approach of learning by doing also in mind, pupils can be asked to select or design picture postcards they might choose to send to particular recipients to project an idea or image.

CONCLUSION

Encouraging pupils to be observant, to look for patterns in what is observed, to set up hypotheses, and to move from observation and interpretation through a thinking rationale to explanation, are approaches common to many school subjects. In history teaching today, appropriate visual material can be incorporated alongside written sources in the study of many personalities or events. Visuals can be used in each of the principal approaches commonly adopted in secondary school history teaching: line of development, patch history, local history, and contemporary history. By looking at a variety of media, visual literacy can be fostered and children made aware of the possibilities and limitations of each form. The increased availability of visual sources has occurred at a time when history teaching has become more child-centred, with emphasis on the pupil's own investigations of the past and the use of a broad range of contemporary evidence. Given the evocative nature of much visual material, the view that 'for younger children at the earlier stages of exploration ... the pictorial document (is) more satisfying than the manuscript' is persuasive.(124)

Yet severe limitations exist in using visual evidence, and it would be short-sighted not to acknowledge that in many instances it may not be possible to precisely attribute a particular work or to be certain as to the factors that led to its production. Similarly, it may not be known how some visuals were received by contemporaries, most obviously for the earlier periods of history. A close study of visual evidence seems to support the view of Lowe that

> *the myth which haunts much history teaching, that visual evidence is necessarily simpler than documentary, must be dispelled once and for all.(125)*

Optimum use of visuals in school necessitates some appreciation of the principal stages in the development of perception and creativity. The value of visuals as historical evidence is increased when they are placed in context by accurate dating and attribution and when associated with contemporary written accounts. Although a visual, for example a still photograph, may provide a symbol for an age, it is important to enquire of the evidence, 'Is it true?' and to demonstrate the risks of being deceived by an image which may have been 'staged'. Only by linking a visual with other illustrated or documentary sources can the problems of bias be fully comprehended.

There are advantages in 'learning by doing', so that the practice and the discovery of visuals can go hand in hand, facilitating the interaction between historical scholarship and the creative spark. The analytical and critical perception of visual evidence should ideally be accompanied by the recording, transcription and reconstruction of history in a variety of graphic and visual as well as the written forms, an approach in which photography can play an increasingly important role in the secondary school.

The choice of visuals for children of top primary and early secondary school level should present few difficulties, for at this age pupils are often avid collectors - stamps, postcards, medals, old coins - and are already beginning to develop their own classification systems. Similarly, the observation and recording of slight differences between two illustrations is popular in the leisure reading material of both children and adults, and it is not difficult to set up visual comparison exercises in the teaching of history. Presenting pupils with groups of illustrations and asking them to match and look for similarities and differences can assist in pattern recognition and the identification of pattern break. Establishing patterns of similarity can assist in developing the concept of order - continuity; looking for differences may help to pinpoint innovation or change, a break in pattern which can spark off historical inquiry. Presenting children with the unexpected, a mystery or puzzle to be solved, is likely to arouse considerable curiosity, stimulated not by similarities but by differences.

The study of art forms gives a greater understanding of the epochs in history. The history teacher may find it particularly useful to consult the works of recognised art historians before attempting to introduce a visual dimension in which iconography and allegory represent significant elements. For example, in looking at portraits of the sixteenth and seventeenth centuries, it may be helpful to study the works of David Piper or Roy Strong; and Hogarth engravings cannot be fully appreciated without reading Ronald Paulson. Where there is no guide from art history, the 'rationale for looking' may prove a useful starting point. Although the primary task of the history teacher will be to use the visual dimension as evidence for investigation and explanation, students can also be aided in their aesthetic education, for history is a particularly rich subject in illustrating the artistic development of society.

The usefulness of illustrations in textbooks and library books is lessened if they are reproduced without comment and, unfortunately, sloppy caption work is still too common. Captions can be a valuable aid to observation and should not be just included as an afterthought. The inclusion of such detail as identification, classification, dating and attribution should be normal publishing practice if visuals are to be treated as sources of information from which students can learn. Similarly, where line drawings and artistic imaginings are included, it would assist history teachers if some indication was given of how they have been produced, possibly by the inclusion of one or more items of visual or written evidence on which the reconstruction is based. The careful integration of illustrations and text should be standard practice.

Finally, a cautionary note is necessary. Important as visual stimuli are, it would be a mistake to ignore the function of words by themselves. Although visuals may seem to be essential for the proper communication of ideas and for a comprehensive understanding of certain subjects, there are topics in history for which neither illustration nor decoration may be necessary or appropriate.

NOTES ON THE TEXT

1 M.J. Broadbent, 'History Books for Schools: 28', *History* 56 (1971).

2 H. Trevor-Roper intro., *The Age of Experience* (1968).

3 N. McCord, 'Photographs as Historical Evidence', *The Local Historian* 13 (1) (1978).

4 L. James, *Print and the People 1819-51* (1976).

5 D. Hartley & M. Elliot, *Life and Work of the People of England*, 4 vols (1929).

6 A.E. Wolfe Aylward, *The Pictorial Life of Wolfe* (1927).

7 A. Wraight & V. Stern, *In Search of Christopher Marlowe* (1965); H. Kraus, *Sir Francis Drake: A Pictorial Biography* (1970).

8 H. & A. Gernsheim, *A Concise History of Photography* (1965).

9 A. James, *Charles Nègre, Photographer 1820-80* (1963); J. Harper & S. Triggs (eds), *Portrait of a Period: A Collection of Notman Photographs 1856-1915* (1968); R. Greenhill, *Early Photography in Canada* (1965).

10 McCord, *op.cit.*

11 M.E. Bryant, 'Sight and Sound in History Teaching', *History Today* 21 (March, 1971).

12 J. Wilkes, 'Under-utilisation of audio-visual aids: some comparative evidence from history teachers in Northern Ireland', *British Journal of Educational Technology* (1977).

13 For examples of other pamphlets see Historical Association, *The Use of Film in History Teaching (TH37)* (1972); *Heraldry (TH38)* (1978).

14 R.W. Southern, 'The Historical Experience', *Times Literary Supplement* (24 June 1977).

15 *Ibid.*

16 Sir K. Clark, 'The Study of Art History', *The Historical Association 1906-56* (1956). Lecture for Jubilee Meeting.

17 *Ibid.*

18 Quoted in D. White, 'Art and the Social Scientist', *New Society* (21 September 1978).

19 E. Gombrich, 'Art versus History is No Contest' (1975).

20 *Ibid.*

21 For the development of these ideas see E. Gombrich, *The Sense of Order: A Study in the Psychology of Decorative Art* (1979).

22 White, *op.cit.*

23 J. Berger, 'Courbet and the Visible', *New Society* (19 January 1978).

24 R. Paulson, *Emblem and Expression* (1975).

25 D. Piper, 'The Portraits of Charles I', in C.V. Wedgwood, *King Charles I* (1949).

26 M. Soames, *Clementine Churchill* (1979).

27 H. Wölfflin, *The Art of the Italian Renaissance* (1903).

28 E. Gombrich, *Norm and Form* (1966).

29 G. Lapage, *Art and the Scientist* (1961).

30 F.D. Klingender, *Art and the Industrial Revolution* (1947, rev.ed., 1972).

31 B. Nicolson, *Joseph Wright of Derby*, 2 vols (1968).

32 P. Fuller, 'Mighty Opposites', *New Society* (22 June 1978).

33 J. Farrell, *The Dark Side of the Landscape* (1979).

34 N. Tucker, 'Ways Children See', *Times Educational Supplement* (3 November 1978).

35 H. Eng, *The Psychology of Children's Drawings* (1931).

36 R. Kellogg, *Analysing Children's Art* (1969).

37 J. West, 'Young Children's Awareness of the Past', *Trends in Education* (Spring, 1978).

38 *Active History* (1972): Booklets by J. Platts, including *Saxon England; Vikings; Norman England; Medieval England: The Country; Medieval England: The Town.*

39 *Patterson Blick Instant Picture Books* including *Waterloo (22); Ancient Egypt (23); D-Day (24).*

40 See *Heraldry and worksheets* (Historical Association, *Teaching of History* series *TH38* (1978); P. Martin, *Heraldry* (1979).

41 M. Buckels & B. Scott, 'A Patch Study in a Junior School Using Monumental Brass Rubbings', *Teaching History* 3 (11) (1974).

42 F. Burgess, 'Spoils of Time - Churchyards and Education', *Amateur Historian* 6 (7) (1965).

43 *History Through Portraits* (colour film *TE229* from FLTE).

44 F. Stadlen, 'Pictures as Propaganda and Historical Record', *Times Educational Supplement* (18 January 1974).

45 A. Booth, 'What Gives a Picture Pupil Appeal', *Educational Studies* 1 (1).

46 M. McNeil, *How Things Began* (1975). Review by M. Booth in *Teaching History*.

47 P. Carpi (ed), *The Book of Art* (1979).

48 *History* 14 (1929).

49 See, for example A. Sorrell & A. Birley, *Imperial Rome* (1970); T. Cairns, *The Romans and Their Empire* book two in *The Cambridge Introduction to the History of Mankind.*

50 S. Sancha, *The Castle Story* (1978).

51 D. Macaulay, *Castles* (1978).

52 G.I. Goder, 'Priemy Raboty S. Uchebrioi Kartinoi', *Prepodavanie Istorii v. Shkole* 4 (1964).

53 Buckels & Scott, *op.cit.*

54 *Ibid.*

55 West, *op.cit.*

56 M. Auer, *The Illustrated History of the Camera: 1839 to the Present Day* (1975).

57 *Ibid.*

58 R. Laurance, 'Images of the Future', *Times Educational Supplement* quoting P. Cummings, the AEB's chief examiner for photography.

59 McCord, *op.cit.*

60 M. Langford, *Basic Photography* (1974).

61 For examples see H. Evans, *Pictures on a Page* (1978).

62 G.C. Dickinson, *Maps and Air Photographs* second ed. (1979); S. Booth, *The Aerofilms Book of England from the Air* (1979).

63 For example, photographic collections for a single county include: B. Berryman, *Scarborough As It Was*; G. Capel, *Harrogate As It Was*; H. Speak & J. Forrester, *Old Wakefield in Photographs*; R. Willis, *York As It Was* (1972-73).

64 See D. Steel & L. Taylor, *Family History in Schools* (1973); D. Steel, *Discovering Your Family History* (1979); S. Purkis, 'An Experiment in Family History with First Year Juniors', *Teaching History* 4 (15) (1976).

65 See O. Aston, *Time and Change* (1973).

66 See M. Hiley, *Victorian Working Women* (1979).

67 A.B. Craven, *Victorian and Edwardian Yorkshire from Old Photographs* (1971).

68 *Ibid.*

69 C. Obolensky (compiler), *The Russian Empire: A Portrait in Photographs*, intro. M. Hayward (1980).

70 *London Street Scenes 1875: Street Traders, Transport, Shops and Poverty, Amusements, Advertising and a Street Doctor* (Slide Centre, 1978).

71 H. Gernsheim, *Creative Photography: Aesthetic Trends 1839-1960* (1961).

72 R. Strong in his foreword to *Beaton Portraits* (1968).

73 E. Gombrich, J. Hochberg, M. Black, *Art, Perception and Reality* (1973).

74 See for example, D. Piper, 'The Portraits of Charles I' in C.V. Wedgwood, *King Charles I* (1949); D. Piper, 'The English Portrait', *History Today* 5 (1955); D. Piper, *Catalogue of Seventeenth Century Portraits in the National Portrait Gallery 1625-1714* (1962); R. Strong & J. Oman, *Elizabeth R* (1971); R. Strong, *Holbein and Henry VIII* (1966); R. Strong, *Portraits of Queen Elizabeth I* (1962); R. Strong, *Tudor and Jacobean Portraits*, 2 vols (1969); R. Strong, *Van Dyck: Charles I on Horseback* (1972); R. Strong, *And When Did You Last See Your Father? The Victorian Painter and British History* (1978).

75 R. Strong, *Tudor and Jacobean Portraits.*

76 D. Piper, 'The English Portrait', *History Today* 5 (1955).

77 See M. George, *English Political Caricature: A Study of Opinion and Propaganda*, 2 vols (1960).

78 F.D. Klingender (ed), *Hogarth and English Caricature* (1944).

79 L. James, 'Cruikshank and Early Victorian Caricature', *History Workshop Journal* 6 (1978).

80 *Ibid.*

81 Paulson, *op.cit.*

82 R. Samuel, 'Art, Politics, and Ideology', *History Workshop Journal* 6 (1978). For a discussion of the medieval device of 'antithesis' see P. Burke, *Popular Culture in Early Modern Europe* (1978).

83 R. Paulson, *Hogarth: His Life, Art and Times* (1971).

84 *Ibid.*

85 Quoted in *Autobiographies of Boyhood* (n.d. Blackie).

86 H.M. Atherton, *Political Prints in the Age of Hogarth* (1973).

87 M. George, *op.cit.*

88 H. Mitchell, 'Art and the French Revolution', *History Workshop Journal* 5 (1978).

89 P.L. Curtis, *Apes and Angels: The Irishman in Victorian Caricature* (1971).

90 *Ibid.*

91 *Ibid.*

92 See D. Read, *Edwardian England* (Historical Association, 1972).

93 *Ibid.*

94 See F.E. Huggett, *Victorian England as Seen by Punch.*

95 S. Smith, 'Some Aspects of 1903: A Source Pack Based on Cartoons', *Teaching History* 3 (1974).

96 M. McCarthy, 'Political Cartoons in the History Classroom', *History Teacher* 11 (1) (1977).

97 A. Caiger-Smith, *English Medieval Mural Paintings* (1963).

98 C. Grossinger, ' English Misericords of the Thirteenth and Fourteenth Centuries and their Relationship to Manuscript Illuminations', *Journal of Warburg and Courtauld Institutes* 38 (1975).

99 A. Shickman, '"Turning Pictures" in Shakespeare's England', *The Art Bulletin* (April, 1977).

100 See J. Lewinski, *The Camera at War* (1979).

101 See P. Hodgson, *The War Illustrators* (1977).

102 *Ibid.*

103 Quoted in Evans, *op.cit.*

104 *Ibid.*

105 *Ibid.* Techniques such as painting-out cluttered backgrounds are also common when prints are to be used in newspapers and magazines. In J. Morrison, *The Media Men*, an example is cited of a photograph of the Chinese leadership with the purged members neatly brushed out.

106 *Ibid.* Evans quoting T. Hopkinson, Editor of *Picture Post.*

107 J.A.S. Grenville, *Film as History: the Nature of Film Evidence* (1971).

108 C.H. Gibbs-Smith, *The Bayeux Tapestry* (1973).

109 *Ibid.*

110 D. Gifford, *The British Comic Catalogue 1874-1974* (1975). See also A. Aldridge & G. Perry, *The Penguin Book of Comics* (1967).

111 D. Kunzle, *History of the Comic Strip 1: The Early Comic Strip. Narrative Strips and Picture Stories in the European Broadsheets c.1450-1825* (1973).

112 *Ibid.*

113 Gifford, *op.cit.*

114 J. Feiffer, *The Great Comic Book Heroes* (1965).

115 For the 'probe' approach see R. Wake, 'History as a Separate Discipline: The Case', *Teaching History* 3 (1970).

116 L.S. Mercier, *The Picture of Paris* (1929).

117 W.S. Sparrow, *Advertising and British Art* (1924).

118 C. Gleisner, 'Urban Studies: "Good News" and "Bad News" in a Nineteenth Century Town', *History in School* 3 (1977).

119 E.M. Kauffer, *The Art of the Poster* (1924).

120 See J. Berger, *Ways of Seeing* (1972).

121 L. DeVries, *Victorian Advertisements* (1968).

122 For postcards see R. Carline, *Pictures in the Post* (1971); T. & V. Holt, *Picture Postcards of the Golden Age*.

123 F. Staff, *The Picture Postcard and Its Origins* (1965).

124 J. West, *Archives in School* (Schoolmaster Publishing Company).

125 R. Lowe, 'Local History in the School Curriculum', *The Local Historian* 12 (1976).

APPENDICES

APPENDIX A: FROM OBSERVATION TO EXPLANATION

Look at the two illustrations of street scenes overleaf.

1. What are the illustrations?____________________

2. Who do you think produced the illustrations?____________________

3. Put a circle around the date shown in the chart below when you think the illustrations were taken.

ILLUSTRATION (TOP)	*1850*	*1900*	*1950*	*1970*
ILLUSTRATION (LOWER)	*1850*	*1900*	*1950*	*1970*

4. Which illustration (top or lower) shows the earlier scene?____________________

   Give reasons for your answer____________________

5. List as many differences in the pictures as you can by completing the chart below.

OBJECT	*EARLIER PICTURE*	*LATER PICTURE*
Street	*Cobbled surface*	*Tarmac surface*
Telephone boxes	*Not there*	*Located in middle of the square*
"Wonderland" building	*Located to the right of the square*	*Not there*

6. List as many similar things in the illustrations as you can.

Photographs of the same part of a town at different points of time provide opportunities for demonstrating continuity and change as shown in the two views of Fitzalan Square, Sheffield

7. What questions would you like to ask about the pictures?
   Make a list below.

i) ______

ii) ______

iii) ______

iv) ______

v) ______

vi) ______

vii) ______

viii) ______

8. There were <u>many</u> reasons why the changes shown in the two illustrations took place. Can you list <u>some</u> of the reasons?

______

______

______

9. Which of these reasons do you consider most important in explaining change?

______

______

______

10. What kinds of evidence would you use to test your explanation?

______

______

______

11. Describe how you would use the evidence to test your explanation?

______

______

______

12. When would you be satisfied with the explanation you have reached?

______

______

13. What factors might lead you to change your explanation?

______

______

Contrasting views of factory conditions. A winding room of a cottom mill (1820) suggests a benevolent employer (nurse on the right; children appear relatively well fed and clothed; straight posture). A harsher view is shown in an engraving by Thomas Onwhyn (c.1820-86) from *<u>The Life and Adventures of Michael Armstrong</u>* *(1840) by Frances Trollope.*

APPENDIX B: DETECTING POSSIBLE BIAS

Look at the two illustrations.

1. What are the illustrations?

____

____

2. Who do you think produced the illustrations?

____

____

3. Are there any similarities in the two scenes?

____

____

4. In which mill would you have preferred to work, and why?

____

____

____

5. Make a list of all the differences you can find in the illustrations.

____

____

____

6. List any questions you would like to ask about the illustrations.

____

____

____

7. How do you account for the differences between the illustrations?

____

____

8. Where could you find additional information to help you decide which of the illustrations was nearest to the truth?

____

____

9. What would you look for in a 'balanced' piece of evidence?

____

____

APPENDIX C: WORKING ON A HISTORICAL PROBLEM

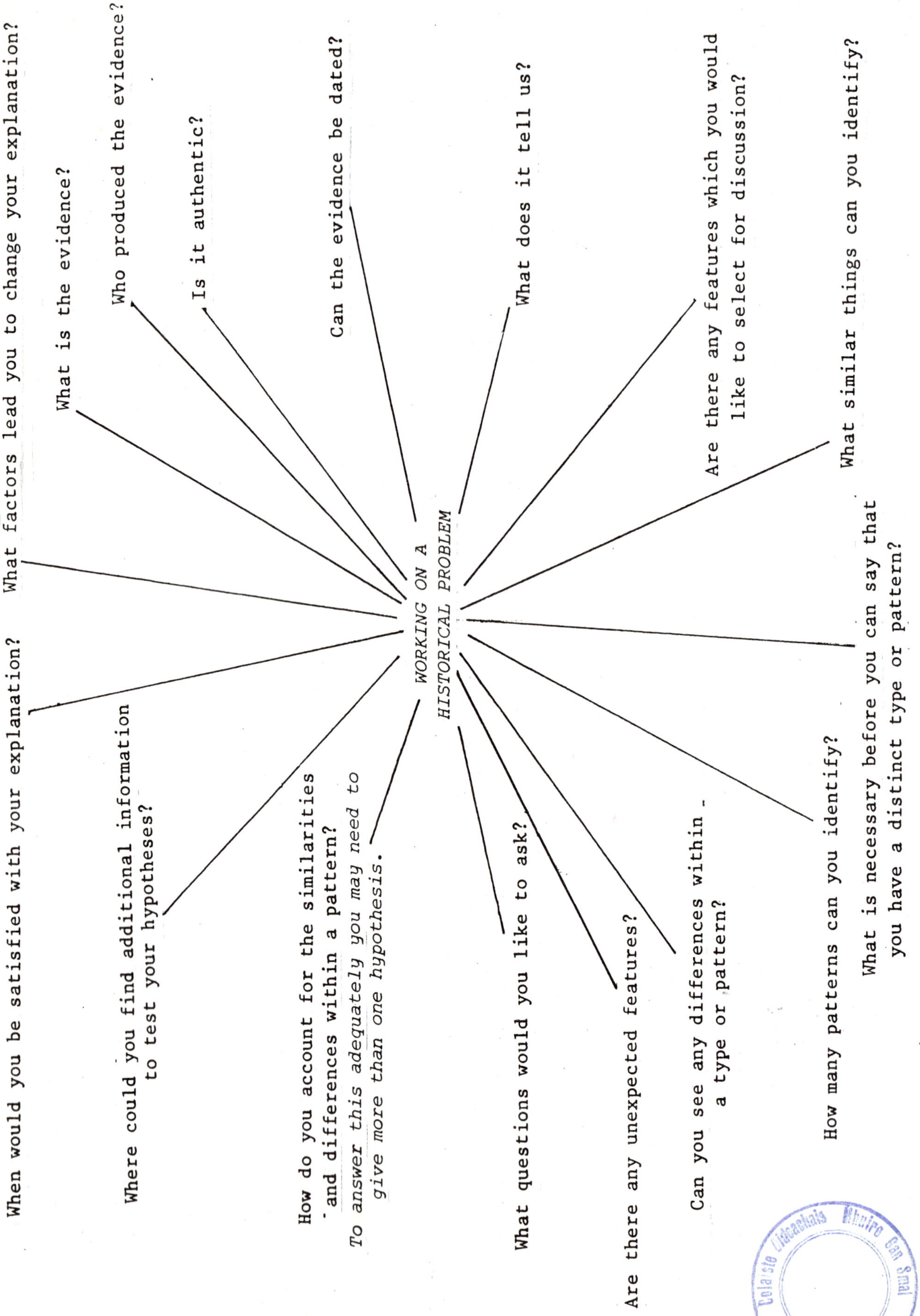